Icons of
RENAISSANCE
Architecture

Alexander Markschies

Icons of
RENAISSANCE
Architecture

Prestel

Munich · Berlin · London · New York

The publisher and author wish to thank those who provided pictures and kindly supplied helpful information, in particular Arnold Bartetzky, Guido von Büren, Dagmar Eichberger, Wolfram Günther, Matthias Müller and Gyöngyi Török. Special thanks also to Dietrich Erben for casting a critical eye over the manuscript.

front cover: detail of façade, Santa Maria Novella, Florence
(Leon Battista Alberti; see p. 22; photo: Alexander Langkals, Landshut)

back cover: top row, from left to right, Hieronymite Monastery of Belém, Lisbon, Portugal (p. 44), Santa Maria della Consolazione, Todi, Italy (p. 52), Juleum, Helmstedt, Germany (p. 132); (bottom row, from left to right): Château of Blois, Loire Valley, France (p. 64), Hampton Court, Richmond upon Thames, England (p. 62), The Old Registry, Bruges, Belgium (p. 86)

frontispiece: detail of floor, Biblioteca Laurenziana
(Michelangelo Buonarotti; see p. 70)

The Library of Congress Cataloguing-in-Publication data is available.
The Deutsche Bibliothek holds a record of this publication in the Deutsche Nationalbibliografie; detailed bibliographical data can be found under:
http://dnb.ddb.de

Prestel books are available worldwide. Please contact your nearest bookseller or one of the following Prestel offices for information concerning your local distributor:

Prestel Verlag
Königinstrasse 9
80539 Munich
Tel. +49 (89) 38 17 09-0
Fax +49 (89) 38 17 09-35
www.prestel.de

Prestel Publishing Ltd.
4 Bloomsbury Place
London WC1A 2QA
Tel. +44 (020) 7323-5004
Fax +44 (020) 7636-8004

Prestel Publishing
175 Fifth Avenue, Suite 402,
New York, NY 10010
Tel. +1 (212) 995-2720
Fax +1 (212) 995-2733
www.prestel.com

Translated from the German by Paul Aston, Dorset
Copyedited by Christopher Wynne
Picture editing by Sandra Leitte

Design and layout: Ulrike Schmidt
Origination: ReproLine, Munich
Printing and binding: Graspo, Zlin

Printed in the Czech Republic on acid-free paper
ISBN 3-7913-2841-7

CONTENTS

INTRODUCTION

The term Renaissance is used these days to describe a period in the history of art, architecture and culture that began shortly after 1400 in Florence and was succeeded by the Baroque style around 1600 – a period characterised primarily by the rediscovery of classical antiquity. As understood by the contemporary artist and writer Giorgio Vasari (1511–74; cf. p. 112), the Renaissance was a revival of the arts after a period of decline in the Middle Ages. New life had been breathed into the classical arts of painting, sculpture and architecture in the late 13th century and, in an uninterrupted process of development, reached perfection in the 16th century.

Although antiquity provided the principal impetus for the Renaissance, in the 15th and 16th centuries the awareness grew that it could be surpassed – that something new, something unknown to the ancients could evolve. In 1598, the French scholar Louis le Roy boasted of the advances of the age, citing in particular the discovery of unknown oceans and lands and new inventions such as printing, gunpowder and compasses. Along with a retrospective view of antiquity, innovation was a second basic characteristic of the Renaissance. In the 15th and 16th centuries, the Egyptian myth of the phoenix rising out of the ashes was often cited to describe contemporary times.

fig. 1. Portrait of Filippo Brunelleschi, from: Giorgio Vasari, *Lives of the Most Excellent Italian Arcitects, Painters and Sculptors*, 1568

ingenious kinds of masonry and their proportions and clearly recognised the special characteristics of the orders.'

Classical architecture was studied even in the Middle Ages. An English scholar called Master Gregory, for example, proudly wrote in the 13th century that he had measured the length of the Pantheon with his own hand. However, its influence became paramount only in the Renaissance. Thus, in a contract for the architectural detail of the crossing piers in St Peter's in Rome (p. 108), it was stipulated that the capitals of the Pantheon be the model on which to base the dimensions and design.

The Leading Role of Architects

Architects played a considerable role in the development of the Renaissance and, in many respects, gave the period its visible face. No other era in the history of architecture has given rise to a comparable wealth of work by outstanding individual personalities, ranging from the Florentine architect Filippo Brunelleschi (fig. 1; cf. pp. 14, 18), who is described as the 'father of Renaissance architecture', to the Italian Carlo Maderno (c.f. p. 108), the Frenchman Salomon de Brosse, the German Elias Holl (cf. p. 136) and the English architect Inigo Jones (cf. p. 138) at the end of the period.

Brunelleschi is thought to have gone to Rome with the Florentine sculptor Donatello in the early 15th century to study classical buildings. In a biography of him written around 1480, it is said that Brunelleschi studied 'almost all buildings in Rome and many in the vicinity' to discover the techniques and stylistic rules used to build them. 'He investigated the excellent and

fig. 2. The interior of the Pantheon in Rome, built between 118-225 AD, and used since 609 AD as a Christian church

Moreover, another work in Rome, the Tempietto at San Pietro in Montorio (p. 42), is one of the first buildings in the history of architecture to draw on antiquity for the building type as well as the detail.

The revival of classical knowledge during the Renaissance meant not only the study and adoption of classical models or even the reconstruction of classical monuments, but also the maintenance of a degree of detachment from them. Though architects took great trouble to reproduce classical architecture in their drawings, they also changed it in their pictorial representations. Francesco di Giorgio (1439–1501), for example, drew the interior of the Roman Pantheon around 1486 and did not hesitate to vary both the proportions and the sequence of supports and apertures in the wall (figs 2, 3). The columns and pilasters of the elevation and the coffering in the roof are tidied into vertical sequence here, i.e. the elevation is systematised. In effect, this is a criticism of the architecture of antiquity – the draughtsman was showing how the building ought to have been built. This critical look at antiquity, whereby models are not taken over blindly, was also characteristic of the sciences – right from the first the Renaissance treated its study of antiquity as an exploration that was both broad and critical.

Few building designers of the 15th and 16th centuries can be considered architects in the modern sense. Many of them – including di Giorgio and Raphael (1483–1520) – had trained as painters, Michelozzo di Bartolomeo (cf. p. 16) completed an apprenticeship as a sculptor, while the most famous of them, Brunelleschi, had qualified as a goldsmith. A background of this sort gave them the competence to design as well as plan the building work and to carry it out – all skills that go into the construction of any building. Others, meanwhile, were trained as masons in the medieval tradition, so they knew all about the handling of materials. Although there was no clearly defined training for architects, at least the ideal of the 'modern architect', i.e. someone who knows his theory and has practical talent, had been formulated in writing. In 1550, Vasari wrote: 'When theory and practice are united in one person, the ideal condition of art is attained, because art is enriched and perfected by knowledge, the opinions and writings of learned artists have more weight and more credit than the words or works of those who have nothing more to recommend them beyond what they have made, whether it be done well or badly.' Architects such as Leon Battista Alberti (cf. p. 20) and Brunelleschi correspond to this ideal. In the biography of Brunelleschi mentioned earlier, which incidentally provides near-contemporary evidence of his high social standing, it is stated: 'At a tender age Filippo learnt to write, read and calculate, as most boys of good families are expected to do in Florence and he also had some book learning.' A sound education enabled Brunelleschi to study mathematics and geometry, while his discovery of central perspective was pioneering for the history of the fine arts.

Written Sources of Renaissance Architecture: The Role of Architectural Treatises

No previous age had seen as many works written about architecture as the Renaissance – thanks pricipally to the invention of printing in 1440. Notable works included Alberti's *De re aedificatoria* (10 vols, 1485; cf. p. 20), the first volume of Sebastiano Serlio's *Regole Generale di Architettura* in 1537 (cf. p. 94) and Giacomo Vignola's *Regola delli Cinque Ordini* in 1562 (cf. p. 110). The latter was the first example of a completely new kind of literature. It remained current as an architectural manual until the 19th and to some extent the 20th century. Even as modernist an architect as Bruno Taut (1880–1938) learnt the basics of architecture from it.

Vignola's book – initially accompanied by lavish engravings – explained *inter alia* the five orders: Tuscan, Doric, Ionic, Corinthian and Composite (fig. 4). Particularly momentous was his thoroughly pragmatic suggestion that the proportions of a building be determined from the overall dimensions according to a modular system relating to the diameter of the columns.

The key source for Vignola – as indeed for all architectural writers of the modern era – was Vitruvius (born *c.* 84 BC), the author of the ten books of *De Architectura*, the only surviving architectural treatise of antiquity. Particularly important was Vitruvius's idea of distinguishing the orders not only formally but also according to their character. The unadorned, austere and ponderous Doric order is thus especially suited to the classical god of war, Mars. Roughness and hardness are the qualities of the simplest order, the Tuscan, which Inigo Jones used for the sake of economy in his church of St Paul's in London's Covent Garden (1631). The use of orders enabled architects to give their buildings a quasi-musical key, ranging from the severe and heavy to the slender and ornately decorated (pp. 20, 82). Since, for example, the west façade of the Louvre in Paris contains only Corinthian and Composite orders, it was obvious to any educated contemporary that the building he was looking at was one of the highest status and import.

Architectural writing in the Renaissance period began with the humanist Jean Martin's translation of Vitruvius (published in 1547), illustrated by the Rouen-born sculptor Jean Goujon (*c.* 1510 – *c.* 65). This work no doubt inspired the gallery in the ballroom of the Louvre (fig. 5; cf. p. 96), which is supported by female caryatides – the history of caryatides going back to Ancient Greece. During the Persian wars, the women of the Spartan city of Caryae had opposed the Athenians. After the destruction of the city, the victors erected a memorial in which support was provided not by columns but by statues of women, the women of Caryae who had been taken captive. France was thus appointing itself a successor to the classical empire of Greece. This is also a reminder that in the Renaissance, not only Roman antiquity was drawn upon as a source.

fig. 4. The five orders of columns explained by Vignola

fig. 5. Caryatides, from Jean Martin, *Architecture*, Paris 1547

In 1567 came Philibert de l'Orme's (cf. p. 98) major written opus, the first book of *L'Architecture*. This series was the only 16th-century treatise written by a non-Italian on the general principles of architecture. It is most informative to compare this with Andrea Palladio's *Quattro Libri dell'Architettura* (cf. p. 120) printed in 1570. This likewise illustrates the construction of buildings from the foundations to the roof.

Finally, the two-volume work by Jacques Androuet du Cerceau (c. 1520–c. 84), *Les plus excellents Bastiments de France*, published in 1576 and 1577, represents a contemporary critical appraisal of French château architecture in the 16th century (cf. p. 94).

Other architectural treatises served as pattern books. An important example in this connection is the series published from 1565 by Hans Vredeman de Vries (1526–1609), which brought Flemish Renaissance architecture to Central Europe and the whole Baltic region. Familiarity with it explains numerous details, such as the gables of the Great Armoury in Gdańsk (p. 134), to mention just one example.

The Contractor as Architect

In his famous architectural treatise, Philibert de l'Orme wrote: 'We have sufficiently advised the architect and the Seigneur, or whoever would like to build, of their positions and duties as the two principal heads of the building enterprise. It remains to turn our pen to the third class of persons, without whom no building can be perfect. These are the master masons, the stone cutters and the workmen, whom the architect must always supervise.'

Numerically, bricklayers and masons, craftsmen, mortar-makers and other labourers certainly constituted the largest group of people among those participating in the construction of a building. A medium-sized palazzo in Florence, for example, employed between 200 and 400 people a year and the construction of the Town Hall in Augsburg in *c.* 1615/16 involved some 550 building workers.

The oddity is that architectural treatises virtually never mention the fourth group without whom no building could ever have been constructed – the contractors, who ran the financial side and organised the construction of a building without acting as clients themselves. Informative in this respect is the career of Hieronymus Lotter (p. 104). Lotter had acquired an immense fortune through financial and mercantile dealings, and was for twenty-seven years a member of Leipzig's City Council, eight times heading it as mayor. Yet recent research would appear to indicate that he never provided drawings or architectural designs.

Lotter's part in the construction of the Town Hall in Leipzig was to organise it and he probably advanced the cash as a loan so that construction work could get underway. No doubt he ultimately took his fair share as well. Alongside him, councillors Hans Cantzler and Hans Volckmar were appointed as overseers. The city ledgers provide comprehensive information about the other principal parties involved in the construction. For example, the head of the carpenters' guild was Hans Hecker, while the rougher stonemasonry work – such as on the steps – was carried out by Peter Pursch. Documented as a bricklayer is Sittich Pfretzschner, whose foreman was the stonemason Paul Speck, who probably also supplied architectural drawings. But even today, it is Lotter whom many still consider the architect of the building, not least because of the legend associated with him. In 1557, he had a document deposited in the tower of the Town Hall that states *inter alia* that he 'presided over' the building and was its 'architectus'.

Things were not so very different at the Château of Fontainebleau in France (p. 76). Here, too, the minutiae of construction work were recorded and we have estimates, contracts, inspection reports and numerous invoices. The leading stonemason, Gilles Le Breton (cf. p. 76), was responsible for the entire operation and all architectural work and, in addition, supervised the purchase of building materials, scaffolding and tools and controlled the labour side. The same legal status was accorded the principal carpenter, roofer, joiner, glazier and locksmith. Moreover, there were the Italian artists, who were mainly responsible for the interior of the château. Their number included Francesco Primaticcio (1504/5–70) and Vignola, who in 1540 had obtained a number of original Ancient Roman sculptures as well as some plaster casts. The designs for the architecture of the château were in all probability made by a certain Pierre Paul or even the patron himself, Francis I.

The Patron as Architect

Very many more people than is generally realised were responsible for planning and constructing a building. Any one of the designers, clerks of the works, organisers or financiers could be termed architect, not least because the precise definition of the architect's role only came much later. Occasionally even the person who commissioned the work took on the role. It is recorded that Federico da Montefeltro, for example, the builder of the late 15th-century Palazzo Ducale in Urbino (p. 26), was 'an admirable architect'. Similarly, it was said of Cosimo de' Medici and his grandson Lorenzo that they 'had built many churches and monasteries and numerous houses' – just as a client would say even today that he had 'built' such and such. In 1585, Giovanni Paolo Lomazzo wrote of the French king Francis I (reigned 1515–47; cf. pp. 64, 76, 96): 'We read that the king frequently took a pen in his hand to practise drawing and painting'. A stained-glass window shows him in the guise of the patron saint of architects, the Apostle Thomas, holding a builder's T-square in his hand as an attribute (fig. 6). Sometimes these tributes were really just fulsome flattery of the client, but in the case of Archduke Ferdinand II of Tyrol the ruler is indeed documented as having furnished designs for a building drawn in his own hand (p. 102).

Of course, artists and architects of the early modern era were almost entirely dependent on there being well-heeled clients and patrons who both wanted and could afford the magnificent works they produced. Vasari's vita of painter and sculptor Antonio Pollaiuolo (1433–98) clearly indicates the link between artists and patrons: 'He led a very happy life as he found rich popes and his native city Florence was at the peak of its prosperity and so could find pleasure in his work. He was also greatly honoured thereby, because in unfavourable times he would not have reaped such fruits.'

Very few written documents of the Renaissance provide information about what motivated clients to spend so much on architecture. Perhaps the most telling example we do have is by Giovanni Rucellai (pp. 20, 22), who sets out his motives: 'All my building commissions have given and still give me great satisfaction and the greatest contentment, since they redound to the glory of God and the honour of the city and my memory'. The Florentine merchant even commissioned a portrait of himself against a background showing the principal buildings he had financed – the Palazzo Rucellai with the loggia in front, a chapel copying the tomb of Christ in Jerusalem and the façade of Santa Maria Novella (fig. 7). These remained a permanent memorial to him, and his works acquired a political and social dimension.

It is worth bearing in mind the famous thesis of the cultural historian Jacob Burckhardt (1818–97) to the effect that in the 15th and 16th centuries art could be created 'for its own sake'. Current scholarship is investigating how buildings could depict meanings within social constellations – Heidelberg Castle (p. 54) and the churches of the Jesuit order (pp. 124, 130) are outstanding examples of this.

One of the most fascinating patron personalities of the Renaissance was the Hungarian king Matthias Corvinus (1443–90). It was through his agency that the new Italian style first acquired its broad European dimension. His court historian Antonio Bonfini (1434–1503) wrote succinctly that he 'brought the architecture of the ancients back into the light'. Matthias invited Italian artists to his court, who worked on sculptures and paintings as well as a number of illuminated books for him that were the wonder of contemporaries. A list of the buildings commissioned by him along with their interiors would fill books, although as a result of the disastrous 150-year Turkish occupation of much of Hungary from 1526 few of these buildings have survived. Even so, the remains are impressive enough. The fragments of the architectural decoration at the royal

fig. 7. Francesco Salviati (attrib.), *Giovanni di Paolo Rucellai*, early 16th century

palace in Buda or the summer palace in Visegrád are qualitatively among the best architectural ornament ever produced in the Renaissance (fig. 8). Matthias's principles of artistic patronage were imitated by later rulers, such as Sigismund I of Poland (p. 66), Francis I of France and the Holy Roman Emperor Charles V (pp. 74, 78). All of them used art to make political statements. It was thus the demand by clients with agendas that gave rise to the fascinating panorama of the Renaissance in Europe.

The Planning and Construction of Buildings in the Renaissance

It may come as a surprise that the process of constructing a building in the Renaissance was not so different from today's. Unless it was an existing building being reconstructed, the first thing was to find a site, level it and lay the foundations. As in the case of the Medici (p. 16) and Strozzi palaces in Florence, even such preparatory measures could cause a stir. The excavations were described as 'magnificent to look at', though a resident complained about all the onlookers and the constant dust in the air. Eventually the foundation stone was laid – on 6 August, 1489 – and a certain Tribaldo de Rossi who was passing that way was asked by the client, Filippo Strozzi, to toss stones and coins on to the site, while his sons scattered rose petals.

It was the client who normally appointed the architect, although sometimes he was selected by holding an open competition, for which design proposals had to be submitted. Competitions of this sort are known to have taken place to find an architect for the construction of the dome for Florence Cathedral (p. 14) for Antwerp's Town Hall (p. 116) and the Great Armoury in Gdańsk (p. 134).

As in the Middle Ages, the principal planning medium in architecture was the drawing, but architectural models acquired increasing importance (cf. p. 39). These allowed the function, structure and effect of the architecture to be checked on a three-dimensional object long before work began. The relationship between windows and rooms could be examined and even matters of internal lighting studied. Models also provided a durable record of the architectural design and were to some extent immune from changes. Thus, given the very lengthy time taken to construct a building, they represented a kind of visible commitment.

Renaissance Architecture Today

Not one of the buildings presented here has survived unchanged. In some cases, such as the Great Armoury in Gdańsk, they were reduced to bare walls in World War II (fig. 9). But previous centuries have also left their mark. The Château of Blois (p. 64) was long used as a barracks, during which time the sculptural decoration was largely destroyed and walls and staircases removed to allow for new room arrangements. In 1843, the château was in a bad way, as one of the earliest architectural

fig. 8. Red marble fragment from the portal to King Matthias Corvinus's palace in Buda, c. 1479

photographs anywhere testifies (fig. 10). In subsequent years it was restored following the precept of the celebrated pioneer restorer of historic monuments, Eugène Viollet-le-Duc (1814–79): 'Restoring a building does not mean maintaining or repairing, it means leaving it in a perfect condition such as possibly never existed at any moment.' Logically, therefore, the restoration of 1844–48 entailed adding a gallery in front of the ground floor of the Francis I Wing, which the building is documented as not having had originally.

Just a few years later, the approach to the care of historic monuments changed. Heidelberg Castle, for instance (p. 54), was left in its ruined condition and John Ruskin (1819–1900) became the luminary of a more cautious treatment of monuments. In 1849, he wrote what could be considered a manifesto for the care of monuments: 'Look after your monuments and you will not need to restore them. A few sheets of lead laid on the roof from time to time, a few dead leaves and twigs removed from a gutter will save both roof and wall from ruin. Watch over an old building with anxious care, count its stones like jewels in a crown. We have no right to touch the monuments. They do not belong to us.'

In this book, sixty-three outstanding works of Renaissance architecture in Europe are presented, with a geographical span stretching from Italy to England and from Lisbon to Moscow. All of these structures merit the label 'masterpiece' and, in the 15th and 16th centuries, some of these were even described as 'wonders' of the world. The fascinating panorama of architectural works brought together in this volume is all the more interesting due to the comparisons that can be made between buildings in different countries. Readers may wonder at a number of inevitable gaps such as certain examples of military architecture or such outstanding individual structures as the triumphal arch of Alfonso of Aragon in Naples, the Certosa of Pavia, the Strada Nuova in Genoa or Vadstena in Sweden. The very nature of making a selection means that there always have to be certain limitations.

fig. 10. Blois, Francis I's staircase-tower seen from the courtyard before its restoration. Daguerreotype by Hippolyte Bayard, 1843

FOUNDLINGS' HOSPITAL
(OSPEDALE DEGLI INNOCENTI)
Filippo Brunelleschi

Florence, Italy, begun 1419

Renaissance architecture burst onto the scene with a fanfare in the very first building by the 15th century's most notable architect, Filippo Brunelleschi. The architecture of the Ospedale was greatly admired from the outset. Originally it was a hospital for the poor and the sick. It became known as the Foundlings' Hospital because abandoned infants could be handed in at a small revolving door that still survives. Fourteen glazed terracotta medallions by Andrea della Robbia depicting infants recall this function of the hospital with graphic vividness.

All architectural features of the façade are made of a fine sandstone with a greenish sheen, whereas the wall surfaces are plastered white. A low flight of steps leads up to broad, spacious colonnaded loggia. The ground plan is not new; what is new is the architectural treatment. The loggia is distinctive for its use of the grammar of classical antiquity. For the first time for centuries, columns were once again a main design feature.

One of the architect's innovative ideas was, however, not carried out. The pilasters on the end bays were to have been continued to the upper storey. In the event, only the wider gap between the windows above the pilasters indicates this earlier plan.

A glance at the ground plan of the building shows other refinements in the artistry of the design. New in terms of architectural history is the symmetry of the plan. The central doorway leads into a quadrangle and, unlike in the cloister garth of medieval monasteries, the doorway is placed centrally, not at the corners. In fact, the inner courtyard appears to establish the axis of symmetry of the ground plan, and the most important functional units, the church and the great hall of the hospital, are orientated to it accordingly. The concept of a regularised ground plan was to become a core feature of Renaissance architecture.

In 1401, Brunelleschi is thought to have travelled to Rome with Donatello to study classical sculpture and architecture. However, the main inspiration for the Foundlings' Hospital came from Florentine architecture of the 11th and 12th centuries, the 'Proto-Renaissance'. Immediate models in this style for Brunelleschi were notably the Cluniac Church of San Miniato al Monte and the Baptistery. It is still a matter of debate whether the architect knew these buildings were medieval or thought they dated back to antiquity. Even in the 16th century, many Florentines still thought that the Baptistery had originally been a Temple of Mars built in classical times. In any case, Brunelleschi's Foundlings' Hospital and Old Sacristy in San Lorenzo draw much more heavily on medieval architecture than is generally supposed.

Plan of the ground floor

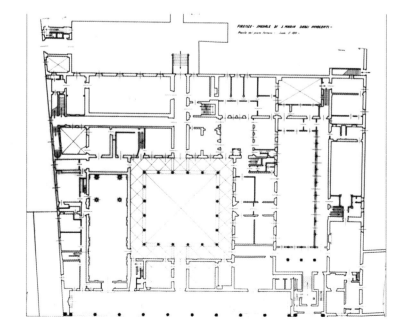

Filippo Brunelleschi

1377   Born in Florence as the son of a notary
1401   Probably goes to Rome with Donatello and studies classical art
1403   Takes part in the competition for the second bronze door of the Florentine Baptistery with a scene of Abraham sacrificing Isaac
1404   Qualifies as a master goldsmith
1419   Begins work on the cupola of the Cathedral of Santa Maria del Fiore, Florence
1429   Completes the Old Sacristy of San Lorenzo, Florence
1446   Dies on 16 April in Florence. His death mask has been preserved

The loggia with terracotta reliefs depicting foundlings added to Brunelleschi's tondi by Andrea della Robbia in 1487

View of the loggia from the Piazza Santissima Annunziata

The inner courtyard (the Men's Court)

PALAZZO MEDICI
Michelozzo di Bartolomeo

Florence, Italy, begun 1445

A high point of quattrocento architecture in Florence, the Palazzo Medici (later known as the Palazzo Medici-Riccardi) possessed all the features that a lavish private residence of its day required. It was in a prominent location and dominated neighbouring buildings. Moreover, in its architectural expression, it also documented the Medici claim to power as the leading family in the city.

It already caused a stir when the foundations were being laid, but the most telling comment came from Pope Pius II, visiting Florence in 1459 shortly after the building was completed, to the effect that the palace was worthy of a king. In the same year, the Milanese duke Francesco Sforza received a letter saying that 'if Your Eminence could see the palace, I am sure the sight of it would cost You a pretty penny. Because on seeing such expenditure and liberality You would also set to work on a similar scale, not just to equal but to surpass the model, if that were possible.'

These remarks sum up not only the exterior of the building, such as the façade, where the rustication on the ground floor recalls the walls enclosing the Roman Forum of Augustus – considered at that date to have been an imperial residence. The splendid interior court with its adjacent garden also attracted attention. But above all it was the works of art put on display here that obviously made the biggest impression, including the Judith and Holofernes group by Donatello dating from 1456/57. The relief medallions over the arcades of the court were inspired by classical models in the possession of the Medici.

In the 15th century, high-ranking visitors were received not at the entrance to the palace, but, as they were later in Baroque times, at the top of the stairs to the upper residential level. From here one entered the palace chapel, where the panel painting by Filippo Lippi and the frescoes by Benozzo Gozzoli are among the glories of quattrocento painting.

The architect of the palace was Michelozzo di Bartolomeo. An earlier design by Filippo Brunelleschi was not carried out, as it seemed too large and too lavish. With Florence nominally a republic, the Medici always had to be careful not to create the impression of striving for autocracy.

After 1670, seven bays were added to the main façade and a gallery was then added to the interior, which the Baroque painter Luca Giordano (1634–1705) decorated with frescoes. This turned the Palazzo Medici into a Baroque city residence.

Michelozzo di Bartolomeo

1396	Born in Florence, the son of an immigrant tailor from France
1410–47	Employed as a die-cutter in the mint
1417	Works with Lorenzo Ghiberti on the bronze doors of the Baptistery in Florence
1419	Joins forces with Donatello, with whom he works on four joint projects
c. 1420	First commissions from Cosimo de'Medici – the church of San Francesco in Bosco ai Frati and a villa
c. 1436	Reconstruction of part of the church and monastery of San Marco, Florence
1444–	Tribune of Santissima Annunziata, Florence
1472	Dies on 7 October

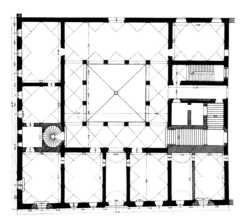

Ground plan

Ferdinando del Migliore, view of the palazzo prior to the Baroque extension, 1684

Both family seat of the Medici's and administrative centre: the Palazzo Medici-Riccardi on the Via Cavour

right: Detail of a window

far right: The inner courtyard

SANTO SPIRITO
Filippo Brunelleschi

Florence, Italy, 1446–1482

The Florentine Church of Santo Spirito is Brunelleschi's most impressive building. Externally it is the huge dimensions of the building that impress. Inside, it is the harmony of the proportions, the even lighting and the uniform design, down to the last detail.

The architect did not live to see the church completed. The first column was delivered to the site on 5 April, 1446, shortly before he died and was left there untouched for eight years, during which time work was suspended.

If an architect dies before construction work readily gets going, it is never certain that his plans will be carried out in the way he intended. Whether Brunelleschi had had a different exterior for the church in mind or planned a different roofing system, such as a barrel vaulting, continues to be debated. Nothing survives of his plans, either as drawings or as an architectural model.

And yet it is assumed that the building was constructed largely according to the architect's intentions. It is, after all, one of the finest churches of the quattrocento. The basic aesthetic concept adhered to was laid down by the client, the Augustinians. Like the Franciscans and Dominicans, the Augustinians were a mendicant order – their aim being to live as simply as possible in emulation of Christ. This attitude is reflected in the largely undecorated exterior of the church. In the interior, a ground plan was adopted that was originally developed for the Cistercians back in the 12th century – the St Bernard scheme, named after the most influential abbot of that order, St Bernard of Clairvaux (1090–1153). In this, the square of the crossing becomes the determinant of all other spatial dimensions, including the aisle chapels. Even the centrally positioned column behind the high altar in Santo Spirito followed Cistercian choir principles – usually a choir chapel came here with a centrally placed window. Thus both in its exterior and internal arrangement Santo Spirito is visibly a monastic building.

Stringency and perfection are the guiding principles of the architectural concept of Santo Spirito. That even Brunelleschi could surpass himself is clear from a comparison with a scheme for his earlier major church in Florence, San Lorenzo (from c. 1421 onwards). The columns of the nave are echoed there by pilasters in the aisles, while in Santo Spirito the aisles also have columns. Accordingly Brunelleschi's first biographer, Antonio Manetti, describes the finished church as perfect. Writing in the 1480s, he said that Brunelleschi wanted to put his artistic ideal into practice in the building – and, in historical retrospect, achieved his aim.

The architecture of the church is complemented by panel paintings and sculptures from leading Renaissance artists. They include works by Filippo Lippi, Domenico Ghirlandaio and Andrea Sansovino. Michelangelo is supposed to have executed his first sculptures here, a capital decorated with figures and a crucifix. As part of his aesthetic concept, Brunelleschi also supplied specifications for the interior by allowing only pictures of the same format to be placed in the altars of the aisle chapels.

A high-point of quattrocento architecture is the church sacristy that Simone del Pollaiuolo and Giuliano da Sangallo added from 1488 on the west side. The adjoining barrel-vaulted vestibule is particularly impressive.

Ground plan and cross-section of the nave and sacristy

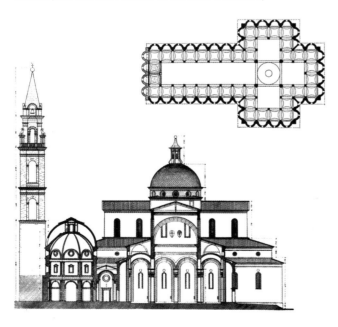

The façade from the Piazza Santo Spirito. The volutes and crowning gable were added in 1758

View of the sacristy located on the west side of the church

View of the nave

PALAZZO RUCELLAI
Leon Battista Alberti

Florence, Italy, c. 1450

The Palazzo Rucellai was the residence of the Florentine wool merchant Giovanni Rucellai (1403–81). Unlike many other prosperous burghers who likewise had residences built, Rucellai wanted not just functional structures, but something that he would be remembered for. He therefore set an extensive building programme in train, including a country house south of Florence and a palazzo in the city itself with a separate loggia, the façade of the Dominican church of Santa Maria Novella (p. 22) and finally an imitation of Christ's tomb as a last resting place for himself. Ambitions on this scale made him comparable in his patronage only with the leading family of Florence, the Medici, especially Cosimo de' Medici.

As with Sant'Andrea in Mantua (p. 28) in the ecclesiastical sphere, Alberti here set new standards with his most famous secular building. Whereas Filippo Brunelleschi's Foundlings' Hospital had introduced an array of columns as a new way to articulate façades (p. 14), the same idea was now carried over to a residential building. Three orders of pilasters were superimposed on the three equally high storeys, echoing the façade typology of classical architecture. The model was the Colos-seum in Rome, which also inspired the system of orders – the simplest at the bottom, the most ornate at the top. The architect's desire to imitate antiquity found further expression in, for example, the moulded architraves of the ground-floor windows and the *opus reticulatum* of the basement façade, a classical technique in which squared facing stones are set diagonally into the wall in a mesh pattern. All elements of the design present alternatives to the traditional grammar of older façade architecture. Contemporaries were aware of this. The architect Antonio Filarete, for example, wrote in 1464: 'The whole front façade is formed of dressed stones and everything is done in the style of antiquity'.

Within Florence, the façade of the Palazzo Rucellai had no successors as it was out of step with current ideas of display, for which the Palazzo Medici (p. 16) was more influential. Outside Florence, it exerted more influence. The Palazzo Piccolomini in Pienza (p. 24), for example, was composed along virtually the same lines, while the façades of the Palazzo Rovere in Savona by Giuliano da Sangallo and various Roman palazzi, such as the Palazzo della Cancelleria (p. 36), were inspired by it.

The Rucellai loggia, 19th-century engraving

Dessein des Loges modernes baties selon les regles de la bonne Architecture, Celle cy apartenoit a la Maison de Rucellai

Leon Battista Alberti

1404	Born the illegitimate son of a Florentine banker on 14 February in Genoa
1420/21–28	Studies law in Bologna
1432–	Secretary at the Papal Curia in Rome
1435	First theoretical work, *De Pictura* (On Painting), the forerunner of other books on sculpture and architecture
c. 1435–40	Designs two bronze medallions bearing his own portrait (Musée du Louvre, Paris, and National Gallery, Washington, DC)
1450–	Practises as an architect, producing plans for at least six buildings
1472	Dies in Rome in April

View of the
façade facing
the Piazza
de'Rucellai

SANTA MARIA NOVELLA
Leon Battista Alberti

Florence, Italy, begun c. 1458

In 1469, the Dominican monk Domenico da Corella (1403–83) wrote a kind of traveller's guide to the principal religious sites in Tuscany (especially Florence) and Rome. Of Santa Maria Novella he states: 'The church is also renowned for its exquisite cloister and the long series of stone vaults which cover it. Although its external appearance was attractive, it could not, unlike the present one, boast a beautiful façade. Inflamed with an intense love for the Holy Mother, Giovanni Rucellai paid for the entire construction with his own money. Thanks to him, the outside of the church is now embellished with a new façade of coloured marble. People praise him to the heavens and duly show him their immense gratitude. To this work is also linked the glory of Battista Alberti, who managed to create it through his art and skill. He adorned the façade with fruit-laden branches that stretch above the church doors and decorated the marble with varied designs. The façade was thus renovated and

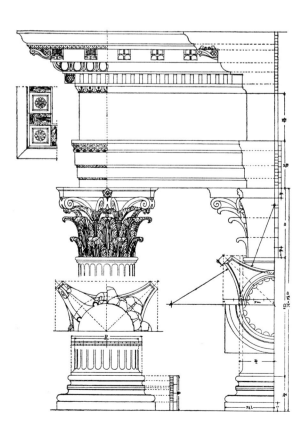

The Corinthian capital from Leon Battista Alberti's major ten-volume work *On Architecture (De re aedificatoria)*

rendered more beautiful, thanks to the ability of this distinguished artist.'

A distinguished theologian, Corella manifests in this description a lively awareness of the church's building history, which goes back to 1248. Planning of the façade commenced around 1300. In the following decades, two sets of three tomb niches with pointed arches were built either side of the main doorway (the side doors in between were also part of the original plan). When Alberti was appointed, he had to take this existing work into account, the donors of the first façade having stipulated that the extant parts of the front should not be changed. They also required the remaining parts of the façade to be decorated with various kinds of marble cladding.

Thus Alberti's façade for Santa Maria Novella is in a very real sense a renovation, as Corella writes. The architectural genius lies in the way it is handled. The degree of Alberti's success is evident not least in the effect the façade had on subsequent architects. His massive upper-level scrolls were copied in churches until well into Baroque times.

Alberti drew on classical sources in designing the façade, direct models also including buildings that, in Renaissance times, were considered to date from antiquity such as the Baptistery in Florence and the Romanesque Church of San Miniato al Monte outside Florence. He furnished Santa Maria Novella with a façade that can be described as a temple front. The lower storey of blind arcading is divided up by four massive engaged columns and framed at the ends by square piers. Above the entablature and four pilasters is an attic storey crowned by a pediment.

The architecture of the central doorway is based on that of the Pantheon in Rome, as is the inscription below the pediment, which gives the name of the donor (Giovanni Rucellai) and the date (1470), although the façade was still documented as under construction in 1478. Rucellai's motives for endowing architecture are known from his writings. He wanted to ensure he would be remembered, to beautify his city and, finally, to demonstrate his piety. His summary is rather rueful: 'For fifty years I have done nothing but make money and spend it, and I have become aware that spending money is sweeter than making it.'

View of the decorated façade from the Piazza di Santa Maria Novella.
The church abuts a graveyard which was consecrated in 1323

General view of the church and monastery

View of the interior

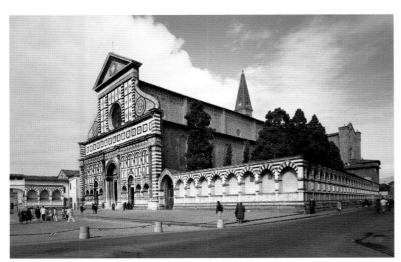

PIENZA
Pope Pius II Piccolomini /
Bernardo Rossellino

Pienza, Italy, begun 1459

Situated south of Siena, Pienza was the first ideal city to be built in the modern era. There is nothing comparable with it in ambition and homogeneity. Its founder was Pope Pius II, the humanist Aeneas Piccolomini (1405–64), whose aim was to rebuild his virtually derelict, native, hilltop village of Corsignano as the 'city of Pius'. In his principal literary work, the *Commentarii*, he writes his purpose in building Pienza was to make it a 'permanent symbol of his origin'.

The Florentine architect Bernardo Rossellino (1409–64) was commissioned to supervise the work, and he was responsible for the central square and its monumental buildings, the cathedral and the pope's private palace. Subsequent additions were the palazzo comunale and a number of buildings for cardinals and the pope's retinue. Particularly impressive is the row of houses erected on the Via delle Nuove Case in the north-east of the city, where twelve houses were built from the 1460s to a standardised plan. They provided accommodation for the families who had lost their homes owing to the rebuilding in the centre of the town. Today they would be classed as council housing.

Pius's own 'Commentarii' form the basis for understanding the historical development of a town. An important consideration for his own residence, the Palazzo Piccolomini, was the possibility of an unobstructed view. The papal residence was therefore developed on the south side as a three-storey panoramic loggia. The decision to orientate the palace to the nearby hills was based on readings of classical authors and this was the first time landscape had consciously been invoked as an experience since classical times. Not much later, the idea was taken up in other buildings, such as the garden wing of the château at Blois (p. 64) or the Villa Rotonda (p. 120).

The interior of the cathedral was modelled on Gothic hall churches that Pius had seen 'among the Germans in Austria'. What he valued most was their quality of light. Recent excavations have uncovered stonemasons' marks that are otherwise found only in the north. Whether the architect Rossellino, who had previously worked in Rome for Pope Nicholas v, had himself ventured north of the Alps is not known. It seems far more likely that in Pienza he put into practice the ideas of his cultured and well-travelled client, seeking actual models in Italian architecture. Just to what extent consideration was being given at that time to different aspects of town planning, can be seen in Antonio Filarete's architectural treatise or the famous series of three views of idealised, stage-like, early Renaissance spaces, probably drafted around 1470 by the circle of artists associated with Piero della Francesca.

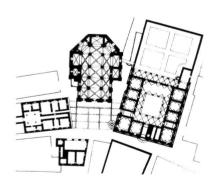

Plan of the buildings around the central town square

Piero della Francesca, *The Ideal City*, Galleria Nazionale, Urbino

Piazza Pio II: the heart of Pienza with the Town Hall, Bishop's Palace ...

... the Cathedral and the Palazzo Piccolomini

PALAZZO DUCALE
Luciano Laurana

Urbino, Italy, after 1465

The first ruler's palace of the Renaissance was built in the central Italian ducal city of Urbino. It was already praised by contemporaries – they compared it with palaces of the Roman emperors and even called it a 'city in the shape of a palace'.

Work began on the new building in the 1450s. From 1466, Dalmatian-born Luciano Laurana (*c.* 1400 or 1420–79), about whom little else is known, took over as architect. The main parts he was responsible for were the courtyard of the palace, its central entrance staircase and the principal rooms. The client was one of the most sought-after military leaders in Europe, Duke Federico da Montefeltro (1422–82). The ruler was also one of the leading art patrons of the day, who employed, for example, Piero della Francesca as a court painter. As he had discovered no painters in Italy who were skilled in the techniques of oil painting, he called in the Netherlandish painter Joos van Wassenhove to paint portraits of twenty-eight famous people for him. These are now among the most important furnishings of the ducal palace.

Written sources indicate that Federico started or continued no fewer than 130 building projects. He was in close touch with Leon Battista Alberti. In his treatise on architecture, Alberti had provided a typological definition of a modern prince's residence, ranking it top in his classification of secular buildings. His ideas had already influenced the construction of the papal palace of Pienza (p. 24). In Urbino, the result was a ducal palace with no fortifications, marking a significant move away from traditional military architecture and helping to establish a satisfactory architectural formula for residences of civil rulers.

The internal arrangement of the ducal palace is notable for wide corridors and ample public rooms, including one of the largest libraries of its day. The duke's apartments form the climax of a carefully planned route for visitors. High-ranking guests passed through grand public rooms and residential areas to reach the confined proportions of the *studiolo* with its splendid inlaid interior depicting Federico's programme as a ruler. From here there was access to a balcony that, as in Pienza, looked out on an impressive landscape. It is even thought that a morning ceremony, like the *levée* later practised by French kings, took place here.

Thus it was not only the building of the Palazzo Ducale that proved pioneering for European palatial architecture. It was also a forerunner of Baroque ceremonial.

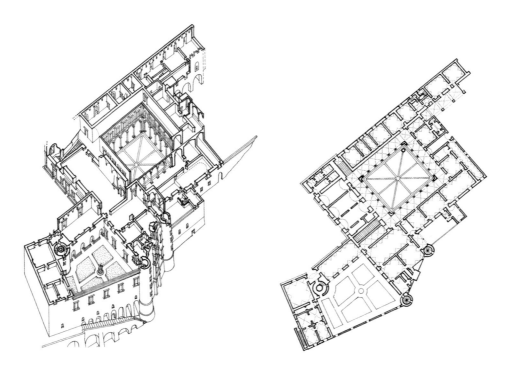

Isometric projection and plan

A 'city in the shape of a palace': the Palazzo Ducale in Urbino

The corridor looking towards the staircase

The inner courtyard (*cour d'honneur*)

SANT'ANDREA
Leon Battista Alberti

Mantua, Italy, planned from 1470

The most important religious attraction in Mantua is a reliquary with the blood of Christ which, until the 15th century, was preserved in a medieval church on the same site that was not at all suited to accommodating large numbers of pilgrims – the Benedictine abbey of Sant'Andrea. To some extent for the sake of prestige, but more particularly for practical reasons, the Margrave of Mantua, Ludovico Gonzaga, commissioned Antonio Manetti to build a new church. The Florentine architect had won his spurs at the celebrated abbey church of Badia Fiesolana in Fiesole. However, the abbot of Sant'Andrea demurred at the idea of rebuilding – in his view the existing church was too venerable to be demolished.

Thus planning was resumed only after the abbot's death. Leon Battista Alberti immediately took the opportunity to put his name forward as architect. In a justly famous letter to Gonzaga dated October 1470, he wrote: 'I have also learned that Your lordship and your citizens have been discussing building here at Sant'Andrea. And that the chief aim was to have a large space where many people could see the Blood of Christ. I saw Manetti's design and I liked it. But to me it does not seem suitable for your purpose. I thought and conceived of this, which I send you. It will be more capacious, more eternal, more worthy, more appropriate. It will cost much less. This type of temple

was called an Etruscan shrine by the ancients. If you like it, I will see to drawing it out in proportion.'

The margrave answered this exemplary letter of application a few days later. He was willing in principle to be convinced, but was unable to imagine exactly what Alberti had in mind. The architect should therefore come to Mantua. Clearly agreement was reached, since not much later work on the new church had already started.

As the margrave wrote, one aim of the new building was to 'honour himself and the city'. The use of a triumphal arch motif for the main front of the church seems specially intended to meet this requirement.

The interior, on the other hand, is a monumental showcase to display the reliquary of Christ's blood and at the same time accommodate large numbers of pilgrims. Over 330 feet long, it is a two-storey, barrel-vaulted church that directs the eye of the visitor from the moment he enters the church towards the high altar, where the reliquary is on display. No other church in the architectural history of the 15th century displays such huge and impressive dimensions. Once again, antiquity was a major source of inspiration, specifically the Basilica of Maxentius in Rome, which served as a model even for the masonry techniques.

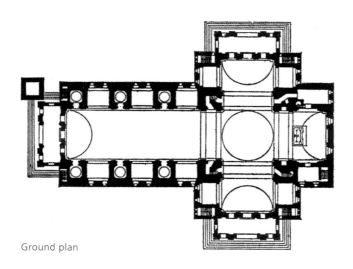

Ground plan

View of what is today the Piazza Mantegna in Mantua. This detail shows the façade of Sant'Andrea, 18th century, Technical University, Berlin (Plan Collection)

The entrance front of Sant'Andrea, for centuries a magnet for streams of pilgrims

The interior, looking towards the high altar where
a reliquary with the blood of Christ is kept

THE KREMLIN
Aristotele Fioravanti and Alovisio Novi

Moscow, Russia, begun 1475

The Grand Prince of Moscow Ivan the Great (1440–1505) reached the zenith of his power in the 1480s. He had freed his city of Tatar subjection and gradually brought various principalities, such as Yaroslavl, Rostov and Novgorod, under his control to form a Russian empire. He emphasised his ambitions by calling himself the 'Autocrat', 'Sovereign of All Russia' and occasionally even 'Tsar'. With his marriage to Sophia, a niece of Constantine Palaeologus, the last Emperor of Byzantium, he also saw himself as a direct successor of the rulers of antiquity. Subsequently he established a central administration, made arrangements for the succession and in 1497 promulgated a general legislative code.

He furnished his seat of government, called the Kremlin like the centres of all Russian cities generally placed on hills, with buildings on a scale unprecedented anywhere in Europe. The task was entrusted exclusively to Italian architects and engineers. Even in the 16th century, the new walls, churches and palaces earned Moscow a reputation as a 'third Rome'.

Work began on rebuilding the walls of Moscow in 1485. Construction was supervised by Pietro Antonio Solari, and after he died, by Alovisio Novi, and also included several new towers. Both men were also responsible for other buildings in the Kremlin. Solari and Marco Ruffo built the Faceted Palace, which served as the throne room and assembly room within the extensive palace complex. Though drastically altered in subsequent centuries, its architecture exhibits a direct link with Italian architecture. The inspiration for the diamond patterning of the exterior was probably the Palazzo dei Diamanti in Ferrara. Novi's Cathedral of the Archangel Michael, built from 1505 to 1509, also followed the model of Italian architecture. The ground plan with its five domes can be traced back to churches built in Venice shortly beforehand, such as San Giovanni Chrisostomo.

Ultimately, of course, the model for the church where the grand princes were buried was San Marco in Venice.

Probably the most famous building in the Kremlin is the Cathedral of the Dormition. Built in the 15th and 16th centuries, it was used for ceremonies of state, such as for the installation of grand princes in office, coronations (from the 16th century) and the funerals of patriarchs. In size and splendour, the cathedral surpassed all other buildings in the Kremlin. Its architect was Aristotele Fioravanti (1415 / 20–85 / 86), who hailed from Bologna. A contemporary chronicle records what seems to have been a very difficult search for a suitable man: 'The Grand Prince sent his envoy Semën Tolbutsin to Venice to visit the ruler. And he gave orders for a church architect to be found. Tolbutsin said there were many artists there, but none was worthy of Russia. Finally agreement was reached with Master Aristotele, who had made, it was said, the gates of Venice; they are fine and imaginative.'

According to everything we know, the report is pure invention. In fact Fioravanti came from the court of Matthias Corvinus of Hungary (cf. p. 11) and was summoned to Moscow as an engineer to extend the fortifications in accordance with the latest military expertise. He was definitely no expert in architectural aesthetics, and perhaps that is why the cathedral has so little obvious connection with Italian architecture. It is more likely that inspiration came from Russian medieval buildings. It is documented that Fioravanti studied the Cathedral of Vladimir at Ivan the Great's behest. In these circumstances, the Moscow building became a virtual copy, only new building techniques rendering it Renaissance architecture – Fioravanti used a compass, spirit-level and drawings. Equally innovative for Russian architecture was the use of bricks and mortar to construct walls.

The seat of government extends over a vast area: view of the Kremlin with its churches and palace buildings

The Cathedral of the Archangel Michael

right:
The faceted palace

far right:
The Cathedral of the Dormition

SANTA MARIA PRESSO SAN SATIRO
Donato Bramante

Milan, Italy, 1478–1523

The church of Santa Maria presso San Satiro is Bramante's principal work in Milan before he left for Rome to design the Tempietto (p. 42) and work on St Peter's (p. 108). As the name indicates, there are two buildings here on one site – the church of Santa Maria and the chapel of San Satiro. The latter is a small, centralised building dating from the ninth century attached to the north transept of the church. It is dedicated to St Satyrus, a fourth-century bishop whose cult is confined to Milan.

As so often, the occasion for building the new church was a miracle-working image of the Virgin (cf. p. 52). The first part constructed was the transept; then, in 1486, work began on the façade under the supervision of architect and sculptor Giovanni Antonio Amadeo (1447–1522). One of Bramante's duties here was to choose the colour pattern for the marble.

The church was finally consecrated in 1523, but the task of laying the marble floor took until 1552. Its present appearance is largely the result of considerable restoration work in the 19th and early 20th centuries, during which the roofs were raised, a new main altar was installed and the church was decorated with paintings. The façade is also new, the original façade design having been implemented only at plinth level, probably owing to funds running out.

The interior of the church reveals a nave-and-aisle ground plan in the shape of a Latin cross, whereby the shallow east end appears as a deep chancel on account of the *trompe l'œil* paintings with which the space is decorated. Behind this, a mere yard or so away, is a street, which prevented the building being extended in that direction. In terms of aesthetics, Bramante treated the nave as a foreshortened design, making use of one of the most important achievements of cinquecento painting, namely the mastery of central perspective. The inspiration for the illusionist architecture might well have been Masaccio's Trinity fresco in Santa Maria Novella in Florence from *c*. 1425.

Artistically, the illusionist chancel was not an end in itself – its principal purpose was to give the impression that the building is centrally planned. Central ground plans were more or less obligatory for all Italian Renaissance churches and many houses of worship north of the Alps dedicated to the Virgin. As a document from 1480 notes, what was desired was a church that 'contributed to the beauty of the city'. This was a requirement of other buildings as well, but was applied here for the first time to an interior, as is evidenced by the *trompe l'œil* architecture, which established the enduring reputation of the church.

From 1483 to 1486, a sacristy was added in the corner between the nave and the south transept of Santa Maria presso San Satiro. In type, it adopts a late classical tradition particularly common in northern Italy. The ground plan displays an octagonal centrally planned design expanded to include alternate semi-circular and rectangular niches. Demonstrating an extraordinary height for its width, the sacristy's impressive interior was subsequently imitated in a whole series of northern Italian churches.

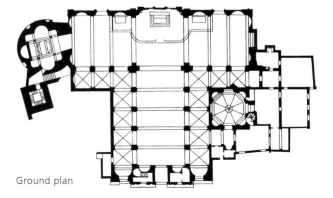

Ground plan

Donato Bramante

1444	Born the son of a shepherd. Trains as a painter and draughtsman, probably in Urbino
1481	First documented work – the Previdari engraving
1482–1500	Works in Milan as an architect at Santa Maria presso San Satiro, Santa Maria delle Grazie, Sant'Ambrogio
1503–	Works for the pope: Vatican palace, St Peter's, Santa Maria del Pòpolo
1504	Completes the cloister of Santa Maria della Pace in Rome
c. 1510	Palazzo Caprini in Rome
1514	Dies on 11 April

View of the group of buildings that make up Santa Maria presso San Satiro: on the right is the Early Romanesque bell-tower, on the left, the chapel of San Satiro and in the background the nave and crossing

below, from left to right:

The entrance front, completed in 1872 to plans drawn by Giuseppe Vandoni

View towards the choir

T.V. Parravicini, *Church façade on the Via del Falcone*, from *L'Architteture del Rinascimento in Lombardia*, Biblioteca d'Arte del Castello Sforzesco, Milan

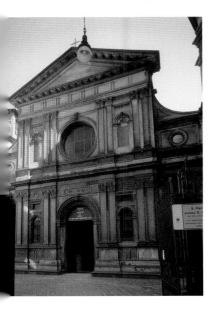

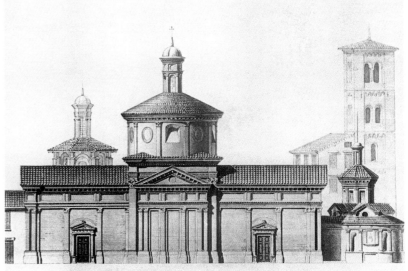

SANTA MARIA DEI MIRACOLI
Pietro Lombardo

Venice, Italy, 1481–1489

That the Miracoli in Venice was an architectural jewel was something already appreciated by 15th-century contemporaries. Deeply impressed by it, the German Felix Faber noted in 1484 that no prince was capable of a work of this kind. Ten years later, an English traveller recalled the profound impact it had had on him, 'the fairest of any Nunnery, for the beauty and rare stones, the walls covered with marble'. And an Italian wrote that this building surpassed any in Venice apart from St Mark's for its cost, artistic perfection and beauty.

As you approach the church, it becomes apparent that it has four fronts of equal status and that all four sides are covered with costly, ultra-thin marble cladding. It looks more like a jewel case than a church. The impression was intentional, since inside the building is a wonder-working picture of the Virgin and Child, and the church was built solely to house it. The use of exquisite varieties of stone was precisely calculated and contractually agreed with the architect of the church even before work began – the contract specified Carrara and Greek marble with striped inclusions and red and black Verona stone, naturally of the highest quality that could be found. The inclusions meant that, if the blocks were appropriately cut, the stones could be laid out symmetrically. Occasionally this produced geometrical patterns or even abstract, ornamental faces. Unfortunately the original fabric of the building was seriously damaged by drastic restoration work undertaken in the 19th and 20th centuries.

The designer of the church, Pietro Lombardo, was mentioned by name in a contract with the convent signed in 1481, where he is described as the sculptor of a tomb for the Doge Pietro Mocenigo in the Venetian Church of Santi Giovanni e Paolo. He was thus not an architect in the fullest sense – clearly those who commissioned Santa Maria dei Miracoli were looking for someone who specialised in stone. Lombardo's qualities as a sculptor can be directly appreciated in the masonry work, which is largely original. The screens around the altar, which were intended to keep the throng of pilgrims from the sanctuary, and the other ornamentation of the building, such as capitals and entablatures, are among some of the finest work done in the 15th century.

Pietro Lombardo

c. 1435	Born in Corona, Lombardy, Italy. He and his family, especially his sons Tullio and Antonio, rank among the most important architects and sculptors in Venice
c. 1470	Embellishes the chancel of San Giobbe, Venice
1476–81	Tomb of Doge Pietro Mocenigo in Santi Giovanni e Paolo, Venice
1480–	Commissions for various tombs in and around Venice: for Jacopo Marcello in Santa Maria dei Frari, Venice, and Archbishop Giovanni Zanetti in Treviso Cathedral
1489	Architect of the Scuola Grande di San Marco, Venice
1515	Dies in Venice in June

Longitudinal section

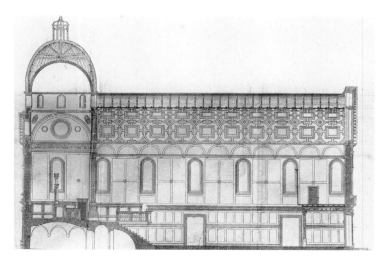

Exterior view of the choir from the adjoining canal, the Rio dei Miracoli

The entrance front from the Campo dei Miracoli

PALAZZO DELLA CANCELLERIA

Rome, Italy, 1488–1496

In 1483, Cardinal Raffaele Riario, nephew of Pope Sixtus IV (1471–84), was appointed titular bishop of the Roman Church of San Lorenzo in Damaso. Originally a fourth-century Early Christian colonnaded basilica, it had, like the attached palace, fallen into a state of disrepair. To clear the site for the grandiose new Palazzo della Cancelleria, begun in late 1488, the church was razed to the ground, though its grey granite columns were re-used for the interior court of the palace. The new church was begun in or around 1493 and was integrated into the palace, which thus assumed gigantic proportions. The church is completely hidden behind the façade of the latter, only the two doorways in the vast façade indicating that separate functions are concealed behind it. The left (grander) door leads to the inner court of the Cancelleria, the right one to the church, which may have been built by Donato Bramante. It is a measure of Riario's sense of power that he dared to hide away one of Rome's title churches behind the ostentatious façade of his private residence, in effect making it a chapel.

The side and rear alignments of the Cancelleria followed the existing street pattern – indeed, the southern (left) end of the palace façade makes an angle of no less than 70 degrees, which had to be coped with aesthetically. The main façade was straightened out with line and plumbline, thus setting a regularised base line for the new, small square established in front. The façade is fourteen bays wide. The end bays are a little broader and project slightly from the rest of the front, representing tentative forerunners of a major design feature in Baroque architecture. Their appearance here marks their first occurrence in palace architecture.

In function and use, the Cancelleria – so called after being used as a meeting place of the papal council – was quite traditional, a typical feature being the numerous shops built into the ground-floor walls at the sides. The combination with a church is also typical of a Roman cardinal's palace. But what the unknown architect of the Cancelleria designed was rather special, in that he followed the most important architectural treatise of the 15th century, Leon Battista Alberti's *De re aedificatoria* (On Building) printed in 1485. There we are told about the most elegant of all palaces: 'It should be situated in the middle of the city, be easy of access and finely decorated, manifesting elegant rather than overweening splendour. In addition, the theatre, the church and the houses of the best people make a splendid ensemble.'

The inner quadrangle of the Cancelleria acts here as the theatre. Its design is based on that of the Palazzo Ducale in Urbino (p. 26), though it is on a much larger scale. Moreover the façade is modelled on that of the Palazzo Rucellai in Florence (p. 20), which can be seen in its superimposed array of pilaster orders, and even in the cut of travertine marble, echoing that of the Colosseum and the Forum Romanum. However, the elevation is different: the Roman version is livelier and more harmonious. The Palazzo della Cancelleria is another gem of quattrocento Roman secular architecture. It dispenses with the hitherto customary fortification features, such as battlements, emphasising instead the elegance of classical façades.

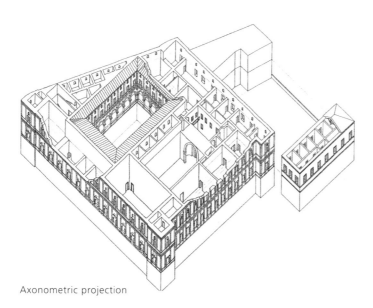

Axonometric projection

View of the main façade of the Palazzo della Cancelleria from the Corso Vittorio Emanuele II

Interior view of San Lorenzo church in Damaso which was integrated into the palace complex

The inner courtyard

PALAZZO STROZZI
Giuliano da Maiano and Il Cronaca

Florence, Italy, 1489–1534

The Palazzo Strozzi is a perfect example of a Renaissance palace, yet its dimensions are unusual. It is based on a ground area of 177 x 131 ft and a height of 100 ft. This made it one of the largest buildings in the city of Florence in the 15th century. Located centrally, on one of the city's most important streets, it is also unusual from a design point of view in that, unlike the Palazzo Medici (p. 16), it has three principal façades. The Palazzo Strozzi is the best documented palazzo of the quattrocento. A reliable fund of sources and a large building model, the oldest surviving model for a private residence in architectural history, shed considerable light on its building history.

The building model was made from September 1489 to February 1490, i.e. shortly after the foundation stone for the palazzo was laid, on 6 August, 1489. It enabled the client, the immensely rich banker Filippo di Matteo Strozzi (1428–91), to get an exact idea of the future shape of his residence, though he himself did not live to see it completed. Like all building models, it also served as a planning medium to judge the effect of the architecture. It could be used to try out spatial and lighting effects, and with a scale of 1:40 it acted as a basis for making templates. Two detailed models that have also survived facilitated discussion of alternative designs for the façade. Much more universal than drawings, building models had become the dominant planning medium in architecture from around the mid-14th century.

Terms used by contemporaries to describe the Palazzo Strozzi were 'beautiful', 'proud' and 'sublime', the principal point of comparison being the Palazzo Medici. Shortly before it was completed, the comparison was tersely summed up thus: 'It will be more splendid'. This corresponded exactly to the motives of the client, who had written in 1474: 'I hope that the things I con-stantly ponder and am constantly planning – assuming God grants me a long life – will ensure my memory.' Thus functional or financial considerations were not particularly important in the construction of the Palazzo Strozzi – the enormous building costs would have sufficed to lease a building for over 3,000 years.

Externally, the design of the palazzo forms a unified whole. Three storeys high and clad with uniform rustication, it is divided into nine window bays on the narrow side and thirteen on the long side. A heavy cornice whose dimensions are tailored to the whole façade provides the conclusion at the top. Three doorways lead into the inner courtyard. With its impressive columns and the architectural detail of the upper storey, the courtyard is one of the finest and at the same time one of the most innovative pieces of architecture in Renaissance Florence. The architect responsible for the interior was Il Cronaca (The Chronicler), so called on account of his comprehensive knowledge of antiquity. The person responsible for designing the exterior is a matter of debate to this day. The model was built by Giuliano da Sangallo (cf. p. 18), one of the quattrocento's leading architects, but, as implemented, the detail so closely follows the Palazzo Pannocchi in Siena, designed by Giuliano da Maiano around 1470, that the inclination is to see him as the architect.

No doubt Strozzi himself played a leading role. In his biography, written towards 1530 by his son Lorenzo, he is even referred to as the architect of the palace. Lorenzo writes that Strozzi had put considerable thought into the appearance of the palace and tried his hand at his own designs. In the 1460s an earlier writer, the architect Filarete, coined a rather apt term for this kind of partnership, saying that buildings had fathers and mothers – patrons and architects.

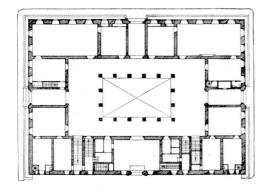

Ground plan

Arguably the grandest and most impressive
Renaissance palace in Florence:
the Palazzo Strozzi

Architectural model

The inner courtyard

VLADISLAV HALL
Benedikt Ried

Hradčany, Prague, Czech Republic, 1493–1502

The rule of the Jagiellon dynasty in Bohemia from 1471 to 1526 remained just an episode of history, yet this was the time when a building of European importance was created through an extensive rebuilding of the Prague Hradčany from the foundations upwards, beginning in 1490. In it is the Vladislav Hall, which has always been considered a notable landmark of its time, and indeed it exercised great influence on 17th and 18th-century architecture in Bohemia, Austria and Germany. The hall was erected at the behest of Vladislav II Jagiello, King of Bohemia and Hungary. The castle had been more or less derelict since the time of Emperor Charles IV (1316–78). The appointed architect was the Austrian-born Benedikt Ried, who had previously been employed as a fortifications engineer in Upper Bavaria.

Ried initially restored the north front of the Hradčany, which is over half a mile long, fortifying it with great round towers called Daliborka and Mihulka. That here a palace was rebuilt as a fortress in the late 15th century while everywhere else castles were being turned into palaces and châteaux is due to the local history. In 1483, the burghers had risen against the king, giving the Hradčany a genuinely defensive function.

The Vladislav Hall was intended as a venue for tournaments, and was therefore astonishingly large – over 200 feet long, 53 feet wide and up to 43 feet high. Still more amazing are features such as the vaulting over five bays that comes down almost to ground level and the large window apertures, which make the room light and airy. The spatial arrangement is quite different from Gothic vaulting, the individual parts of the room running into each other so fluidly that it becomes a single space. The Vladislav Hall is an early example of a 16th-century interior, comparable to the Hall of Antiquities in the Munich Residence (p. 126). The vaulting is more like a sculpture than a roof and has been compared to interlocked and twisted hands.

Technically the structure is also a masterly achievement. Apparently the first bay initially collapsed. Based on improvements to the statics, Ried built the rest of the vaulting so solidly that it even survived a conflagration in 1541, despite burning roof trusses which came crashing down into the room.

Until the early 20th century, the exterior of the Vladislav Hall was considered a later addition after the fire, so marked is the contrast between its Renaissance style and the interior. A dating inscription and other evidence, however, indicate the two were contemporaneous. Probably Ried was adapting an architectural idiom that had become established under King Matthias Corvinus in Hungary towards the end of the 15th century. There was no precedent for secular interiors on such a grand scale, and so, inside, he preferred to stick to tradition, not least because it provided a link with the time of Charles IV, when the magnificent Cathedral of St Vitus in Prague was completed by Peter Parler.

View of Prague, from Hartmann Schedel's *Chronicle of the World*, 1493

Benedikt Ried

1454	Probably born in Ried, Upper Austria
1480–89	Collaborates on the fortifications of Burghausen, Bavaria
c. 1490	First commissions in Prague
1512	Completion of St Barbara's in Kutná Hora
1519–	Various architectural jobs in Bohemia, Moravia and Poland
1534	Dies on 30 September and is buried in St Nikolaus's church in Louny, Bohemia, which he helped to build

The Vladislav Hall where tournaments were once held

View of the exterior

Ground plan showing the vaulting structure

THE TEMPIETTO, SAN PIETRO IN MONTORIO
Donato Bramante

Rome, Italy, 1500

That St Peter was crucified in the vicinity of the Vatican in Rome was known to scholars of the 15th century. Oddly enough, however, the guides to Rome who were supposed to show ordinary pilgrims a route through the city spread the view that the apostle had been martyred on one of Rome's hills, the Gianicolo. The royal house of Aragon took advantage of this legend: in 1480, Ferdinand II founded the new monastery of San Pietro in Montorio on the supposed site of the martyrdom. From 1480/81, work was begun on a church based on a Spanish model, the monastery of San Juan de los Reyes in Toledo, which had just been built.

The place where St Peter was supposed to have been crucified was described by the German Nikolaus Muffel in 1452 as a hole in the ground flanked by two columns. Around 1500, an altar was placed here and only a little later Bramante began work on a building to an extraordinary design, the Tempietto (Little Temple).

Much smaller than it looks in pictures, this round temple is in the confined inner courtyard of the monastery, surrounded by a peristyle of Tuscan columns carrying a Roman Doric entabla-ture. Bramante's original idea of incorporating the courtyard in the aesthetic concept was not realised, for reasons unknown. However, a woodcut from 1540 shows the plan, according to which the whole building would have been surrounded by a loggia.

In his architectural treatise, *I Quattro Libri dell'Architettura* published in 1570, Andrea Palladio treats the Tempietto as a classical building, commenting that Christian buildings put their colonnades inside buildings, the ancients outside. The unique character of the Tempietto could scarcely be better described. It was a type of structure for which post-classical architectural history offered no precedent, so Bramante had little choice but to come up with something new. He therefore resorted to classical architecture, specifically round temple buildings, such as the Temple of Vesta in Tivoli or descriptions of buildings of this type in Vitruvius's books of *De Architectura*. Indeed, there was actually no other way to accommodate a memorial building for St Peter in the confined courtyard of the monastery apart from a round temple. Bramante's design can thus be considered both simple and inspired.

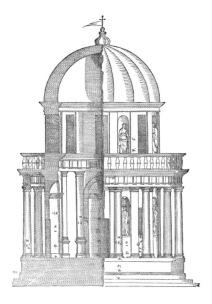
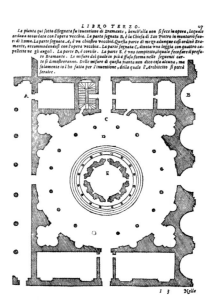

from left to right:

Andrea Palladio, external and internal elevations of the Tempietto, woodcut from *I Quattro Libri dell'Architettura*, 1570

Sebastiano Serlio, ground plan, woodcut from the *Terzo Libro*, 1540

View of the interior

One of the most memorable impressions of Rome: Donato Bramante's Tempietto

HIERONYMITE MONASTERY OF BELÉM
Diogo Boitac / João de Castilho

Lisbon, Portugal, begun 1502

On the night of 8 July, 1497, Vasco da Gama prayed in a small chapel in the former port of Restelo, where the River Tagus runs out into the Atlantic. He hoped for heavenly succour in order to survive a journey into the unknown. Da Gama's aim was to find a sea route to India. His success on that trip turned Portugal into a world power, as his discovery of the East Indies brought immense wealth to the country.

In honour of this event of global importance, King Manuel I of Portugal ('The Fortunate'; 1495–1521) endowed a Hieronymite monastery to be built to replace the old Chapel of Nossa Senhora de Belém dedicated to Our Lady of Bethlehem. The resulting building, which took well into the 16th century to complete, is Portugal's most notable exemple of Renaissance architecture. It survived the terrible earthquake of 1755 only to fall prey to extensive 'restoration' work in the 19th century which greatly changed its external appearance.

The first architect of the monastery was Diogo Boitac, a person about whom virtually nothing is known – for example, it is uncertain whether he came from Portugal or France. The only other documented evidence of him is his work as a fortifications engineer in North Africa. He was followed by João de Castilho, who had completed the cloisters by 1519, considered by many to be among the loveliest in the world.

The architecture of the church, on the other hand, particularly the south front that originally faced the river and has a splendidly ornate doorway, is often considered overbearing and even downright ugly. Criticism of this sort overlooks the historic importance of the monastery and the outstanding quality of the architecture which is based on an overall artistic scheme. The decoration of the interior includes naturalistic motifs, such as ship's ropes, which evoke a 16th-century carvel in stone. The piers supporting the vaulting are dressed up to look like masts with rigging, tackle and sails. As in many other languages, the Portuguese word for nave (*nau*) derives from the Latin *navis*, i.e. a ship, but only in Belém does the word take on a more literal, decorative meaning. The building thus bears unique architectural witness to a time when Portugal was becoming the leading maritime power of Europe.

The maritime motif appears as a metaphor in other Manueline buildings. For example, Tomar Abbey, with its enrichments of the Order of Christ under the governship of Manuel I, is situated on a mountain top and could thus be taken as symbolic of Noah's ark, while the fort in the middle of the Tagus, the Torre de Belém – originally reachable only by boat – resembles a carvel, a traditional sailing ship of the period.

This group of buildings has been termed Manueline in architectural history. Directly associated with their royal patron and momentous historical circumstances, they constitute an idiosyncratic and rather brief episode in Portugal's Renaissance architecture.

Ground plan

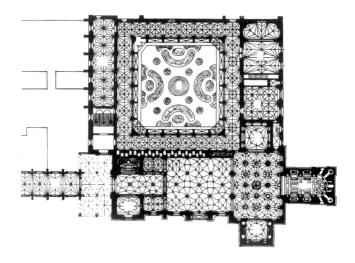

View of the cloisters

The foundation of a 'fortunate' king: the Hieronymite monastery of Belém

The interior of the church

The cloisters

THE WAWEL
Francesco Fiorentino

Cracow, Poland, 1504–1548

The huge pentagonal interior courtyard of the Polish royal palace is a high point of Renaissance architecture in Europe. In its size it is unsurpassed. A novelty here was the first arcaded court north of the Alps. The inspiration for this was Italian – buildings such as the Vatican or the garden façade of the Palazzo Piccolomini in Pienza (p. 24) may have been models. A special feature is the articulation of the elevation: two storeys with columns surmounted by a third storey which has been accorded special treatment in its height and architectural ornamentation. On each section of wall, pairs of columns are placed on top of each other – an idea without antecedent in architectural history. In contrast to French and Italian palace architecture, it was the second floor that thus became the *piano nobile*. Conseuently the representative rooms are also here and not on the first floor as in Italy or France.

Francesco Florentino (as his name suggests, a Florentine-trained architect) began work on the west wing of the new building after the old palace had been largely destroyed by fire. This is where Queen Elizabeth, the mother of the royal patron, Alexander I (1501–06), resided. From 1507, work moved on to the north wing, where Franciscus's fellow Florentine Bartolomeo Berecci was also a collaborator (cf. p. 66). The south wing was added under the latter's direction to complete the enclosure of the courtyard. As there was no space left behind its arcades, this wing remained purely decorative, being built mainly for reasons of symmetry.

Francesco Florentino also produced sculpture for the Wawel, having previously conceived the tomb of King John I Albert (*d.* 1501) for Cracow Cathedral, the earliest Renaissance work in Poland. All that survives of his masonry work for the Wawel are a few unusually splendid window architraves on the third floor of the courtyard. Most doorways were the work of one Master Benedikt from Germany. Unfortunately virtually all the interior furnishings of the Wawel have been lost. These comprised numerous paintings, including one by Titian, ornate floors, candelabras, doors, Venetian window glass and stoves.

In any case, court architecture looked quite different in the 16th century. Strong colours were preferred, the columns for example being deep red. A few much-overpainted frescoes however, do survive, originally painted by Hans Dürer, the famous Nuremberg painter's brother. The best-known interior feature still intact is a ceiling in the Ambassadors' Hall, with some thirty impressively sculpted faces looking down on the viewer.

Cracow was the residence of the Polish kings until 1596, while coronations continued to be carried out in the cathedral until 1734. Following the Austrian occupation in the 19th century wich lasted some hundred years, the royal palace became a national symbol.

General view of the royal palace
on the Wawel

View of the elegant arcades in the inner courtyard of the Polish
royal residence

The ceiling of the Ambassador's Hall. Of the original 194 heads carved
out of limewood between 1531 and 1535, just 30 remain intact

A window surround on the third floor

THE BAKÓCZ CHAPEL

Esztergom Cathedral, Hungary, begun 1506

Although the Renaissance in Hungary is among the most important chapters in European art history, it has only recently attracted the attention it merits. The most important patron in the 15th century was Matthias Corvinus, king of Hungary from 1458 to 1490. As a highly cultured humanist, he encouraged both the arts and scholarship. Earlier than other rulers outside Italy, he commissioned works of art modelled on Italian masterpieces. These include various works, notably the rebuilding of Buda Castle and two villas, of which unfortunately very little has been retained (cf. p. 11). The works of art he commissioned also became famous, such as the magnificent coronation cross in the treasury at Esztergom Cathedral.

Tamás Bakócz (1442–1521) was in some respects Matthias's successor. As primate of Hungary, he also had an extensive collection of books and commissioned buildings such as the chapel now named after him at Esztergom Cathedral which he intended as his last resting place. Despite the vicissitudes of its history – in 1823, when the medieval church of St Adalbert was being rebuilt as a vast Neoclassical cathedral, the chapel was moved stone by stone to a different position – it is among the best-preserved Renaissance monuments in Hungary. The architect remains unknown, but there are good reasons for supposing that it was a colleague of Giuliano da Sangallo, as the ground plan bears a striking resemblance to the Sacristy of Santo Spirito in Florence (p. 18). Likewise the ornamentation, such as the carefully chiselled capitals, recalls works by Sangallo.

The chapel is a square central structure expanded by rectangular niches at the sides. The stone used is red Hungarian marble which lends the interior a warm yet monumental atmosphere. The altarpiece of white marble provides a most unusual focal point. This was made in 1519 by the Florentine sculptor Andrea Ferrucci (1465–1526), whose other works survive in Fiesole, Pistoia and Florence. Despite later depredations – virtually all the figures are missing apart from that of the patron, Tamás Bakócz – it can still be appreciated as a masterpiece of Renaissance sculpture, with ornate foliate ornamentation.

Tamás Bakócz, whose name appears in an inscription of gilt bronze lettering, was born of a serf family and after studying at Italian universities entered the Church, becoming Matthias's secretary, then graduating through the bishoprics of Győr and Eger to the Archbishop of Esztergom in 1497. In 1500, he became a cardinal and, after the death of Julius II, was the losing rival to Giovanni Medici (Leo X) as his successor. His close ties with Italy made the import of Italian art a matter of course.

When it was completed, the chapel was soon lauded as a wonder. 'Everyone who enters it is in transports,' it was said. The architecture and, even more, the sculptural decoration were influential for Hungarian art in the Renaissance as a whole. The artists involved were largely Italian and, in the cultured environment Matthias had created, they obviously stayed on to do other work.

Unfortunately, most of this was destroyed, mainly during the Turkish occupation (1526–1686). Only fragments have survived, some of which are now being restored.

Sectional view of the chapel

Interior view showing
the altar by Andrea
Ferrucio

View of the entrance
seen from inside

The benefactor
Thomas Bakócz's
coat of arms

PALAIS DE SAVOY

Mechelen, Belgium, 1507–1527

A travel book of 1517 states: 'In Mechelen we saw the palace of Princess Margaret, which is fine and well arranged, if not very prepossessing on the outside. Inside there is a well-furnished library for women, and there are wonderful pictures by various good masters.' The author, Antonio de Beatis, shows a clear eye for an interior that obviously took into account the sex of the person for whom it was built.

From 1506, the residence of the dukes of Savoy in Mechelen needed refurbishing when the Duchess of Savoy, Margaret of Austria (1480–1530), was appointed Habsburg regent of the Netherlands by her father, Emperor Maximilian I. This meant in the first place modernising the existing building. Erecting a more extensive palace required the purchase of various plots of land first – what Beatis saw in 1517 describes only an interim state.

The residence was built as a large, four-winged palace in the Late Gothic style. The walls are of brick, the surrounds of the windows and doors of stone. The façade is articulated horizontally with courses of stone. The architecture of the west wing along what is now Korte Magdenstraat has survived fairly well, but the north wing in Keizerstraat was drastically altered by Léonard Blomme in the 19th century. Shortly after the Belgian state was founded in 1830, it was evidently decided that the façade needed a makeover. As historical drawings indicate, it was previously much plainer.

The surviving, largely original lower part of the gatehouse is probably one of the earliest pieces of Renaissance architecture in the Netherlands. It contains a round-arched entrance flanked by pairs of Doric columns, with a pair of niches superimposed between them. We do not know who the architect is, or at least no historical evidence has so far been traced in support of the often-cited Guyot de Beauregard (d. 1551).

The general planning and construction of the Palais de Savoy was in the hands of the Kelderman family, architects and builders, i.e. Mechelen's municipal master builder Anthonis Kelderman I and his son, until 1512–15, and thereafter the new municipal master builder Rombout Kelderman II. Between 1400 and 1550, this family acted as a kind of early capitalist contracting firm involved in building projects in virtually all towns in Brabant (Louvain, Ghent, Brussels, Antwerp, Breda, etc.) and in the northern Netherlands.

Margaret of Austria, the first of three important regents, also commissioned a burial church for herself and her deceased husband at St Niklaas in Brou, near Bourg-en-Bresse. Likewise documented is her involvement in a no longer extant monastery in Bruges.

She furnished her city palace in Mechelen with an art collection of unusual extent and quality for the 16th century. It included, for example, Jan van Eyck's *Arnolfini Wedding* (now in the National Gallery, London). Later the collection was broken up and the interior of the palace rebuilt. However, recent extensive research has enabled the original interior arrangement of the palace to be reconstructed.

Auguste van den Eynde, *The Savoy Court: West Wing seen from Korte Magdenstraat*, Mechelen Municipal Archives

The palace's inner courtyard

The so-called 'New House' situated on the corner of Voochstraat and Korte Magdenstraat, completed in 1512

SANTA MARIA DELLA CONSOLAZIONE

Todi, Italy, 1508

Like many pilgrimage churches, Santa Maria della Conso-lazione is set in a marvellously picturesque landscape. Standing on a slope not far from the gates of Todi, it attracts the eye from far and wide.

The building of the church was prompted by a miracle. According to contemporary legend, in May 1508 two workers looking for building stone discovered an image of the Madonna buried and forgotten in the undergrowth. A miraculous cure was associated with the discovery – one of the workers, who was half-blind, recovered his sight from touching the picture. The immediate consequence was a stream of pilgrims, which in turn made a large church necessary. It was offerings and alms from those same pilgrims that funded it.

Piety alone was not the main reason for constructing the church. In fact, the event was obviously planned – shortly before the discovery of the Madonna, an opening had been made in the city wall to facilitate access to the church site. The miracle probably just served to provide a new source of revenue. Pil-grims were an important economic factor – the principal places of pilgrimage are scattered across the whole of Europe like cus-toms houses.

Like many other pilgrimage churches, the building itself has a central plan, a design that in the Renaissance was thought ideal for a house of worship. For pilgrimage churches dedicated to the Virgin, this particular ground plan was deemed especially appropriate in light of one of the most influential centrally planned buildings in architectural history, the Pantheon of clas-sical Rome, which had been converted into a church dedicated to the Virgin in 609. The ground plan of the church thus carried on a certain tradition.

But the ground plan of Santa Maria della Consolazione also serves to underscore the church's architectural programme. Inside, only one of the altars is dedicated to the Virgin. The others are dedicated to the twelve Apostles, who appear as sculptures in niches behind the altars. Up in the dome above is the dove of the Holy Ghost. The aim of this architectural pro-gramme was to depict the miracle of Pentecost. There is docu-mentary evidence of solemn Pentecostal processions taking place here every year from the 16th until well into the 17th cen-tury. From a theological point of view, the idea was that, after their visit, pilgrims would carry the gospel out into the world.

It is somewhat surprising in view of the clarity of architec-tural purpose that no name of a specific architect has yet been definitively linked with the building. The style is Donato Bramante's and his name is always brought up. Yet he does not feature in any contemporary sources relating to the construc-tion of the church. For want of an alternative, the building is therefore attributed to someone called Cola da Caprarola, of whom we know at least that he thought about the design of steps in the church in 1509.

View of the
high altar

External view of
the pilgrim church

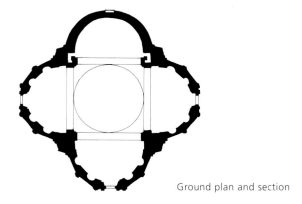

Ground plan and section

HEIDELBERG CASTLE

Heidelberg, Germany, 1508–1632

Although mentioned as early as 1225, it was the building work done during the reigns of Palatinate electors Louis V, Frederick II, Otto Henry and finally Frederick V that turned Heidelberg Castle into a building of European stature. Its glory was increased still further in 1613 by Salomon de Caus's large, lavish terraced garden, the *hortus palatinus*, which in its day was almost as celebrated as the castle itself.

The parts built during Louis V's reign, which include the ladies' quarters, the library with a pretty balcony facing the court, the gate tower of the inner castle and the Brunnenhalle, initially all seem Gothic. They are Renaissance to the extent that new design ideas underlie them. For example, the vaulting of the Brunnenhalle, built from 1510 to 1530, is carried on six granite columns dating from classical antiquity. The re-use of building elements in this way is not uncommon and is intended to add a touch of distinction.

Not much later, Elector Frederick II erected the section in the north-east part of the *enceinte*, the Glass Building, so called

Jacques Fouquières, *Hortus Palatinus*, oil painting, 1620, Kurpfälzisches Museum, Heidelberg

because of the numerous mirrors in the principal room. In style and furnishing, this structure adopted the Italian manner by then established throughout Europe.

The section built during Otto Henry's time incorporates not only Italian but also Netherlandish and French features – for example, the supporting figures of the main doorway are reminiscent of Jean Goujon's gallery in the Louvre (p. 96). The somewhat unbalanced design of the outer wall facing the court with its twenty or so full-length figures reflects a wide-ranging, thematic programme. The statues include Christian and secular virtues, classical deities, Old Testament heroes and a portrait of the patron, Elector Otto Henry.

From 1601 to 1604 the Frederick Building was added by Johannes Schoch for Frederick IV. Like all other buildings in the castle, it is a single block inserted among existing buildings. It adopts the style of the Otto Henry wing but is taller and narrower. The programme of statues is only superficially similar. Here the subject matter is the family history of the new ruling dynasty, the Wittelsbachs of the Palatinate. To this extent, the façade is a response in stone to the Jesuit Church of St Michael in Munich (p. 130).

The English Building in Heidelberg, constructed in the 1610s for Frederick V, has even more intriguing historical associations. The style goes back to English architectural principles, specifically those used by Inigo Jones (p. 138), who is also sometimes cited as the architect of this wing. If that surmise is correct, it can be taken as an indication of the strong connection between the Palatinate and England following Frederick V's marriage to James I's daughter Elizabeth (later known as Elizabeth of Bohemia) in 1613.

The variety and innovative quality of the individual buildings that constitute Heidelberg Castle make it one of the principal works of Renaissance architecture. During the Thirty Years' War and towards the end of the 17th century, the castle was extensively destroyed and subsequently only partly rebuilt. Nonetheless, its still ruinous condition does not impair the incomparably harmonious character of the place.

Bird's-eye view of the castle complex

The Frederick Building seen from the castle courtyard

The façade of the Otto Henry building

VILLA FARNESINA
Baldassare Peruzzi

Rome, Italy, 1509–1511

To this day, the architect Baldassare Peruzzi remains over-shadowed by his more famous contemporaries Raphael and Bramante, even though his two principal works in Rome, the Villa Farnesina and the Palazzo Massimo alle Colonne, are milestones in the history of architecture.

Peruzzi was first active in Siena; why he moved to Rome at the beginning of the 16th century is still not clear. Peruzzi's first architectural job in Rome was the construction of a villa, which has been known as the Villa Farnesina since being adopted as the seat of the Farnese's who lived on the other side of the Tiber (p. 60). It is located beside the Via della Lungara linking the Vatican with Trastevere, which was being developed just as building work began.

Peruzzi constructed the villa as a stately residence in the middle of gardens on the left bank of the Tiber. The client was likewise Sienese, the legendarily rich banker Agostino Chigi (1466–1520). Peruzzi had previously worked for his elder brother Sigismondo on the Villa Le Volte near Siena, which anticipated the main structure of the Villa Farnesina. The U-shaped ground plan, for example, is similar – a feature that would later pass into the idiom of the French château as the *cour d'honneur*.

The Farnesina became famous as a place of prodigious banqueting, where diners ate from gold plates. After the meal, Chigi encouraged guests to throw their plates into the Tiber, whence they were later fished out with nets. Banquets were held against a backdrop of frescoes – prominent works by Raphael and his pupils. The scenes illustrate the horoscope of the master of the house, a cycle depicting the story of Cupid and Psyche and other classical myths. On the upper floor Peruzzi himself executed the paintings for one room, the Sala delle Colonne. The paintings feature trompe l'œil buildings that afford views of the surrounding landscape, and legend has it that even Titian was taken by them. The Villa Farnesina and its decorative programme form a harmoniously integrated whole. A poetic description of it was once given by the great 16th-century architect, painter and artists' biographer Giorgio Vasari, who wrote that the Farnesina was 'not built but born'.

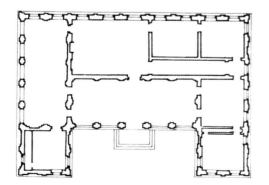

Ground plan

Baldassare Peruzzi

1481	Born on 15 January in Ancaiano, near Siena
1503	Works in Rome, collaboration with Raphael. Assumed to have previously trained as a goldsmith and painter in Siena
1516/17	Painting and architectural work at the Ponzetti Chapel in Santa Maria del Pòpolo in Rome
1518–22	Plans for the church of San Niccolò, Carpi
1520	Begins work on St Peter's in Rome
1532	Palazzo Massimo alle Colonne, his second major work in Rome
1536	Dies in Rome on 6 January and is buried beside Raphael in the Pantheon

View of the villa's south façade

The entrance front facing towards Rome and the Villa Farnesina's principal façade

The garden loggia

The Sala delle Colonne

THE FUGGER CHAPEL
Jakob Fugger and Albrecht Dürer (?)

St Anna's, Augsburg, Germany, 1509–1512

By the beginning of the 16th century, the Fuggers were the wealthiest family in Germany. They financed the politics of popes, kings and emperors. Their patronage of the arts transformed their native city of Augsburg into the first centre of the Renaissance north of the Alps.

One of their principal building commissions was the Fugger Chapel at the former Carmelite Church of St Anna, intended as a family mausoleum for the Fugger brothers Ulrich, Georg and Jakob. It was Jakob ('the Rich') who had the church built and decorated from 1509 to 1512.

The chapel forms the west end of the monastic church, its triumphal arch constituting the termination of the nave. Externally quite unprepossessing; the chapel's glory lies within. The effect must have been much more powerful at the time than now, because until it received a Baroque makeover in the 18th century, the church itself was plain and unadorned. The Fugger Chapel must have seemed higher, brighter and considerably more splendid in contrast.

The interior, with its rib vaulting, patterned marble floor, stained-glass windows, organ with painted wings, choirs stalls and altar, was completed in the late 16th century. The works of art in the chapel include busts made of pear wood for the choir stalls, large marble epitaphs for the Fugger brothers and mourning putti on a screen of columns.

Nowadays the chapel is celebrated as the first example of architecture in Germany in which the idiom of the Italian Renaissance was adopted. Contemporaries were amazed by the richness of the materials used and described the building as unparalleled. The 'fine, large' organ was particularly singled out for praise which, with wings painted by Jörg Breu the Elder, is considered a masterpiece of its day. This enthusiasm overflowed into pictures. Augsburg's art collections possess an unusually large ink drawing in colour showing the chapel in solitary glory, isolated from the church, as if it were a work of art.

However, the lavishness of the work on the Fugger Chapel also attracted critics. A Strasbourg ecclesiastic who cared for the poor of the city asked whether the chapel were of any use to anyone. And what sounds *prima facie* as praise, Ullrich von Hutten's comment that the chapel could have been built by kings, is in fact negative as the patrons were after all only patricians. The context in which the remark was made is also significant, because Hutten (a humanist friend of Luther) was attacking the business policies of the Fuggers, their monopoly of trade, their usurious interest rates and ultimately their influence on the Church.

The square ground plan, architectural balance of the elevations and use of costly materials echo Italian architecture, such as the Church of Santa Maria dei Miracoli in Venice (p. 34). Importing artistic ideas like this allowed the Fuggers to underline the breadth of their cultural horizons and flaunt their wealth. By so doing, they certainly secured long-term prestige for the family and personal fame.

It is still not known who the architect of the chapel was. The name of Albrecht Dürer is frequently put forward, since he is known to have submitted designs for the sculptural decoration. He was a personal acquaintance of the Fuggers, and his architectural depictions in paintings, prints and drawings, or even his ground plan drawings of Venetian palaces, testify to a marked interest in architecture. However, no attribution of the work on the Fugger Chapel has been generally accepted.

Diagrammatic drawing of the Fugger Chapel, signed LS or SL (Sebastian Loscher?), Städtische Kunstsammlungen, Augsburg

One of the putti – originally
six in number – made by the
Renaissance sculptor Hans
Daucher of Augsburg around
1530: this so-called
ercoletto, with its wide-open
eyes, seems to be watching
over the other putti

The Fugger family mausoleum:
the chapel in the monastic church of
St Anna

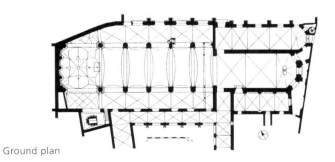

Ground plan

PALAZZO FARNESE
Antonio da Sangallo the Younger and
Michelangelo Buonarotti

Rome, Italy, begun 1514

The Palazzo Farnese is the largest secular building of the Renaissance period in Rome and, thanks to the contributions of architects as diverse as Antonio da Sangallo the Younger and Michelangelo, it also turned out to be one of the most fascinating architectural tales in this city.

The first plans were drawn up in the late 15th century, when Cardinal Alessandro Farnese bought land for the purpose of building a new palace to replace the old cardinal's palace. The purchases were on a grand enough scale to leave room for a large square in front of the future palace.

Building began in 1514, but there were extensive changes of plan in the 1530s and 1540s. A major reason for this was the election of Alessandro Farnese as Pope in 1534. We are told just a little later that the architect 'had to change his original plan in the knowledge that he was building a palace for a pope, not for a cardinal any more. So after demolishing a few neighbouring houses and the old stairwell, he designed a new staircase in which one could go upstairs more easily. In addition, he enlarged the inner courtyard on every side and expanded the palace overall.'

Incomparably more important for the appearance of the palace were the changes made to it after 1546. Obviously the client was no longer satisfied with the upper section of the palace façade. A competition was held for a new design, in which Michelangelo came out triumphant. His interventions concerned the exterior and interior of the palace, and reflect a new view of architecture. For example, Michelangelo had a pioneering idea for the new main window over the entrance door. The opening here is framed by four columns and is, at the same time, set back into the plane of the wall. With its decorative features, it is thus contained entirely within the wall and does not project in front of it, as was normal previously.

In this respect, Michelangelo was treating architecture like a sculptor, as he did at the Biblioteca Laurenziana in Florence (p. 70). His predecessor Antonio da Sangallo the Younger had been much more conventional. The writer and sculptor Benvenuto Cellini said of the latter that his buildings 'lacked true greatness' as he had been neither a painter nor a sculptor and was therefore not an artist in the true sense.

Antonio da Sangallo the Younger

1484	Born on 12 April in Florence. He and his uncles, Giuliano and Antonio the Elder, rank among the principal architects of the 15th and 16th centuries
c. 1506–	Collaboration with Bramante
1513–15	Entrance and courtyard of the fortress in Capodimonte, presumed to be his first independent work
1520–	Architect of St Peter's in Rome (until his death)
1522	Completes the Palazzo Baldassini in Rome
1524–	Works on the Mint in Rome
1546	Dies on 3 August in Terni

Giovanni Battista Piranesi, *Veduta del Palazzo Farnese*, 1773

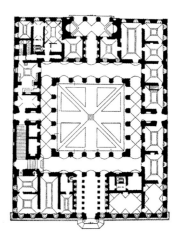

Ground plan

Highly esteemed ever since the Renaissance: the perfect harmony
of the Palazzo Farnese's façade; now the French Embassy

The garden front of the palace

The inner courtyard

HAMPTON COURT
Commissioned by Cardinal Thomas Wolsey and enlarged by King Henry VIII

Richmond upon Thames, England, begun 1514

Located upriver, on the outskirts of modern London, the palace of Hampton Court was one of the largest building projects of the Tudor era. The client was the ambitious Cardinal Thomas Wolsey, a butcher's son who became a prince of the church, papal legate and from 1515 Lord Chancellor. He held the archbishopric of York and numerous other bishoprics, and thereby acquired great wealth which he loved to flaunt.

In 1514 he bought some land by the Thames at Hampton and immediately set to work building himself a palace, starting with the Great Gatehouse with its octagonal corner turrets. Set into the turrets are terracotta roundels containing busts of Roman rulers of antiquity by Giovanni da Maiano. Italian art had now reached England, though in this case in a much purer, small-scale form than in architecture, where imported features long continued to be combined with Tudor Gothic.

The palace was organised into three courts, the Base Court, the Clock Court and the Fountain Court (rebuilt by Sir Christopher Wren from 1689). During Wolsey's time, the wings of the Base Court were erected, serving as accommodation for guests, including the king and his entourage. The king and his queen were provided with two sets of apartments, one above of the other, an arrangement seen earlier in French château architecture. The standard layout of an English palace also included a 17th-century tennis court and a bowling alley.

On 8 August, 1526, Wolsey put on a great banquet at Hampton Court to celebrate the alliance of the French and English monarchs against the Habsburg emperor Charles V. Three years later he fell from power, having alienated the king as a result of the latter's divorce from Catherine of Aragon and having acquired numerous enemies as a result of his policies and arrogance.

A new phase now began in the history of Hampton Court, which passed to the Crown. Henry VIII and his new wife Anne Boleyn rebuilt the chapel and Great Hall. With its spectacular ceiling, the Great Hall is one of the most impressive and largest rooms in the palace. At this date, there were only seven houses in the kingdom large enough to house and entertain the court and its 600-strong retinue.

View of the entrance front of the Tudor palace

Nothing survives of the other rebuildings and the extensive gardens laid out during the reign of Henry VIII. Nonetheless, we know that his new ground plan placed the royal apartments side by side rather than one above the other. In 1529 Henry also had what was called the Bayne Tower built, a narrow, three-storey building that accommodated the Office of the Chamber on the ground floor. Above this, the degree of privacy increased with each storey – the first floor had a bed chamber, a study and a bathroom with running hot and cold water, the second floor a library and jewel house.

General view from the gardens

The Clock Court

Leonard Knyff, *Panoramic View of the Palace in George I's Time (1714–27)*

CHÂTEAU OF BLOIS

Blois, France,
François I Wing, begun 1515

Strategically situated on the Loire, controlling the old road between Bourges and Chartres, the Château of Blois is among the most important buildings of the French Renaissance.

As a fortress, the site was first documented in 903. Of the medieval architecture, mainly parts of the fortifications, a tower and the early 13th-century, two-aisled great hall survive. The French kings Louis XII (1498–1515) and François I (1515–47) both embarked on extensive rebuilding projects at the beginning of their reigns.

Louis XII's work is the central *corps de logis*, or residential block. This major early Renaissance building in France is a stately two-storey edifice principally notable for the colour contrast between dressed stone and red and black brickwork. The size of the apertures indicate that the architecture no longer served any military purpose. Ostentation is now the principal guiding architectural principle, a characteristic feature being the two balconies on the upper storey, or *bel étage*. The one on the right is highlighted by an equestrian statue of Louis XII – though only a poor 19th-century copy survives – the original was destroyed in the French Revolution. Initiated by Marcus Aurelius in Rome (cf. p. 90), equestrian statues advanced to one of the most important demonstrations of power.

The balconies bear witness to an internal arrangement separating the king's apartments from the queen's (Anne of Brittany). We know from a description of the reception of Archduke Philip of Austria in 1501 that the interior was richly decorated with tapestries, precious fabrics, silver lamps, gilt furniture and other valuable items.

The François I wing, on which the new monarch started work immediately after he succeeded to the throne in 1515, introduces an altogether new note – classical architectural features are no longer just decorative elements but integral to the structure as a whole. Above a low basement storey is an accentuated *bel étage*, followed by a second storey with a heavy cornice. The front is divided by supporting pilasters, with a heavy entablature carried right across the façade. Only the central stair tower interrupts the horizontal axis.

The stair tower is the key feature of the building, as the lavish ornamental detail on it emphasises. The panels of the balustrades and supports contain a repeated ornate initial 'F', for François. At ground level, the imperial crown also appears, a clear indication of the king's political ambitions. After the death of the emperor Maximilian in January 1519, François put forward a claim to the Holy Roman crown, as the stair tower documents.

The garden front, which is based on the model of Italian loggia façades, such as those of the Vatican palace in Rome, dates from a later period. Opening on to the garden, it adopts a key feature of Italian residential architecture, enshrining in architectural form the pleasure of looking at landscapes.

The château's central
stair-tower

The Louis XII wing

The loggia façade

Jacques Androuet du Cerceau, the Château of Blois and its gardens,
from *Les plus excellents Bastiments de France*, 1579

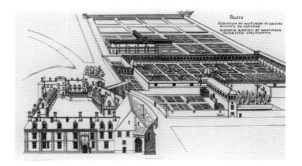

THE SIGISMUND CHAPEL
Bartolomeo Berrecci

Cracow Cathedral, Cracow, Poland, 1517–1533

Around 150 years ago, the Sigismund Chapel in Cracow was described as a 'Renaissance pearl north of the Alps'. In the 16th century, the enthusiasm was much more restrained. Shortly before the foundation stone was laid, the client, King Sigismund I of Poland, wrote: 'An Italian came with the model of the chapel we want to build – and we were very pleased with it.'

The unnamed Italian was probably Bartolomeo Berrecci (c. 1480–1537), a Florentine who trained as a sculptor. The chapel is his magnum opus, since he was responsible for both the architecture and the interior furnishings. Little is known of his life otherwise. It is not even known if he previously worked in Italy or at the court of Matthias Corvinus, King of Hungary. Various sculptures in Cracow Cathedral and the Church of Our Lady are likewise attributed to Berrecci, who probably also played a major part in the works at the Wawel (p. 46).

However, these attributions are surmises, whereas the Sigismund Chapel has an inscription clearly legible in the lantern of the dome that reads BARTOLO FLORENTINO OPIFICE (the work of Bartolomeo of Florence). This is one of the few instances of an artist's signature in Renaissance architecture. Elsewhere, inscriptions on buildings recorded only the name of the client, as, for example, in the courtyard of the Palazzo Ducale of Urbino (p. 26). Thus, enigmatic though he may be, Bartolomeo Berrecci engraved his name for posterity in the Sigismund Chapel.

The chapel is on the south side of the cathedral. The occasion for building it was the death of the Polish king's first wife, Barbara Zapolya. For much of the 16th century the chapel also served as a mausoleum for the Jagiellon dynasty, as Sigismund I, his successor Sigismund II and the latter's sister Anna were later buried here. Like the other sculptures in the chapel, their funerary figures were executed in red marble imported from Hungary. This marble stands out from the grey stone of the chapel to great effect.

The sculpture and architecture of this building are fine examples of Italian Renaissance work. They are based on the chapel architecture of Florence, such as the Gondi Chapel by Giuliano da Sangallo in Santa Maria Novella, and on Roman monumental sculpture, as, for example, in Santa Maria del Popolo. Raphael was another source of inspiration, one of the figures of the very complicated interior programme being based on his fresco of Galatea in the Villa Farnesina (p. 56). The only source of light is the drum of the dome, for which Brunelleschi's dome in Florence Cathedral was the inspiration. Clearly Berrecci was widely versed in Italian art.

Around thirty artists are known to have worked in the construction of the Sigismund Chapel, some even known to us by name. After the work was completed, they remained in the kingdom of Poland to do further work, including some direct copies of the chapel. Their outstanding artistic craftsmanship must have made a great impression, because the Wasa Chapel built in the Baroque period in Cracow Cathedral repeats the exterior of the Sigismund Chapel, even in the detail.

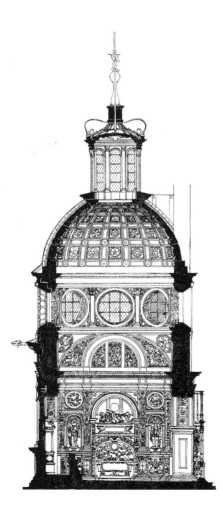

Section of the chapel

View of the cathedral from the south, with the Sigismund Chapel on the right and the Baroque Wasa Chapel on the left

The interior

View of the dome

CHÂTEAU OF CHAMBORD

Loire Valley, France, begun 1519

Francis I's hunting lodge: the Château of Chambord was described as '...the very essence of what human art is capable of...'

When Emperor Charles V visited the hunting lodge of Chambord in 1539, he is supposed to have exclaimed: 'The château is the very essence of what human art is capable of.' Greater praise appears hardly conceivable and yet more informative appreciations do exist. Many a 16th-century contemporary thought that the building surpassed the architecture of antiquity and that it ought even to be counted among the wonders of the world. In 1577, a Venetian envoy described it as 'fabulous', and compared it with depictions of imaginary castles in literature.

This all draws attention to one of the basic features of Chambord. Although at first sight it seems the colossal complex forms a harmonious whole, a closer look reveals certain striking oddities. For example, the windows are a medley of different shapes and sizes, while the roof is a jumble of so many gables, chimneystacks and turrets that one could describe its silhouette as a 'fantasy roofscape'. In addition, the ground plan scarcely catered for the practical requirements of a modern château. Occasionally, Chambord has therefore been considered as the realisation of Utopian notions and more than with almost any other French château, Chambord is directly associated with the pretensions of its builder.

After he came to the throne, Francis I embarked on an ambitious building programme. The starting point was the interior, a central stair tower, from which four equal-sized residential wings radiate. The ground plan is reminiscent of the Castle of Vincennes just outside the gates of Paris, which the Valois king Charles the Wise began rebuilding in 1364. And just as Charles saw his building as a symbol of a divinely appointed monarchy, so Chambord was also intended to assert the universal aspirations of the Angoulême Valois monarchy. The building was, as it were, a monumental advertisement of Francis I's claim to the Holy Roman imperial throne (cf. p. 64); accordingly numerous imperial crowns adorn the central stair tower of the château.

The staircase, an interlocking double spiral, is to be seen as a symbolic axis, allowing free movement up and down simultaneously. This ingenious design is frequently attributed to Leonardo da Vinci, who had come to France at the king's invitation in 1516 and died at the Château of Amboise in 1519. However, no documented connection between Leonardo and Chambord has been found. By way of a footnote, the king himself occupied the château and its 400 rooms for a total of only twenty-seven days.

Double-spiral stair-tower inside the Château of Chambord

Jacques Androuet du Cerceau, ground plan of the château, from *Les plus excellents Bastiments de France*, 1576

View of Chambord's impressive roofscape

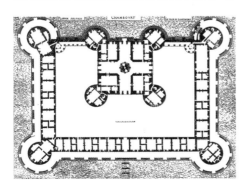

BIBLIOTECA LAURENZIANA
Michelangelo Buonarotti

Florence, Italy, 1524–1571

Directly after he secured the papal throne in autumn 1523, Clement VII – following Leo X, the second Medici pope – decided to build a separate library to house the valuable collection of books his family owned. It comprised some 1,000 volumes and was thus among the largest book collections of the day. San Lorenzo in Florence was the planned location right from the first, as the church was where various members of the family were buried and, by being in the vicinity of the Palazzo Medici (p. 16), it had become a kind of Medici family chapel.

That Michelangelo would be the architect had been settled long before, not least because in 1520 he had designed the New Sacristy, the burial place of the Medici dukes Giuliano and Lorenzo. In January 1524, he wrote to the pope's secretary: 'I learn from your last letter that His Holiness our master wishes the design of the library to be done by me. I have not yet had any communication about this and do not know where he wants to build it. Stefano [the building supervisor of the New Sacristy] related this to me, but I took little heed. Following his return from Cararra, I will ask him about it and do what I can, even if it is not my profession.' This last is an allusion to the fact that Michelangelo considered himself primarily a sculptor, not an architect. Nonetheless, he took the job very seriously and designed the library as pure architecture, without any sculpted or painted finish.

The planning history of the library, named Laurenziana after the great patron of the book collection, Lorenzo de' Medici, is complex, but can be reconstructed with some degree of confidence from the correspondence between Michelangelo and the pope's secretary and from over thirty drawings. Clearly, questions relating to the exact position of the library initially abounded; then it was a matter of the arrangement of the books – should the Latin volumes be separate from the Greek books, or should books of less importance be kept apart from the valuable ones? Additional key planning considerations included the positioning of windows and fire-prevention.

Work began in 1524. By 1526, the actual reading room and the vestibule in front of it, the so-called *ricetto*, were far enough advanced for discussions about furnishings to begin. Then building work was suspended when funds dried up. The solemn opening ceremony did not take place until 1571.

In the meantime, Michelangelo designed the staircase for the vestibule. Built by Bartolomeo Ammanati on the basis of a wooden model, it fills almost the entire lobby. It is the first free-standing flight of steps in an interior, and was often imitated in the 17th and 18th centuries. Michelangelo gave particular prominence to the central flight. As he himself said, this was for the masters, while the side flights were for the servants. The elegant combination of angular and rounded shapes, such as ovals and volutes, was once described as 'a veritable flow of lava'.

The layout of the Laurenziana with a vestibule and reading room is a development of earlier library buildings, such as Michelozzo's work in San Marco, Florence. The harmony of materials (grey-greenish stone for the architectural features and white plaster for the spaces in between) is also typically Florentine, as can be seen on Filippo Brunelleschi's buildings (pp. 14, 18). And yet Michelangelo's work is quite individual. Particularly characteristic is the dynamism of the wall treatment in the *ricetto*. The columns – usually serving as supports – are set in recesses in the wall, eschewing their tradition function as space-fillers. The architectural grammar thus evolved presents a wholly new drama of load-bearing and loads.

Michelangelo's draft sketches

The staircase in the
vestibule of the
Biblioteca Laurenziana

Detail of the stairs

The Great Reading Room:
unlike in later libraries,
books were kept inside
the reading desks

PALAZZO DEL TÈ
Giulio Romano

Mantua, Italy, 1525–1534

A 'villa suburbana': the garden front of the Palazzo del Tè

The Palazzo del Tè got its name from its location – an island south of Mantua called Tè, described in 1492 as a delightful place. Until the early 20th century, it was still only accessible via three bridges.

This was where the builder of the palazzo, Duke Federico Gonzaga, decided to transform the old fortifications and a large stable complex into a 'villa suburbana'. Just like the Villa Farnesina in Rome (p. 56), it was intended as a place for relaxation, celebrations and receptions and was, therefore, not conceived for long stays. The architect of the new project, Giulio Romano, drew on local tradition by imitating military architecture on the long fronts of the four-wing layout, using mock rustication made of brick and plaster. But the *pièce de résistance* of the decorative scheme was the Sala dei Cavalli inside, where the artist painted portraits of horses from Mantua's famous stud farm rather than the usual history paintings or portraits of celebrated personalities.

Giulio worked at the Palazzo del Tè as both architect and painter. Sebastiano Serlio (cf. p. 94) saw the palazzo as the fulfilment of an artistic ideal, citing it as a 'model of our time in architecture and painting'.

Construction probably began in late 1525 and the first rooms were ready by 1528. Subsequently, for reasons not fully clarified, the original plans were expanded, but the additions apparently concerned only the north wing of the present building. Some of the decoration was then finished at high speed to be ready for a visit paid by the emperor Charles V on 2 April, 1530, but despite the haste the building obviously made an impression. The detailed description of his stay mentions that Charles took particular interest in the celebrated paintings in the Sala di Psiche and Sala dei Giganti with its battle of the Titans, and records the Habsburg ruler's enthusiasm for the palace and its decorations. It should be recalled that at the time Charles was busy with his own scheme for a similarly ambitious residence in Granada (p. 74).

In 1533, a Doric frieze was installed in the inner courtyard of the Palazzo del Tè. This is an architectural detail that justly become famous. Parts of the frieze – the metopes – have 'slipped' out of position, with the stones threatening to fall. This would seem to be prevented merely by the diagonal cut of the stones. As if in response, the keystone above the aperture is raised, seemingly prising open the pediment. Features of this sort are indicative of an architectural idiom that relies on there being someone receptive to such effects and conceits.

With the construction of the Palazzo del Tè and rebuilding of the ducal palace and cathedral, Mantua became a noted artistic centre in the first half of the 16th century. With his building commissions, Duke Federico Gonzaga was following a tradition of artistic patronage started by his great-grandfather Ludovico in employing Leon Battista Alberti (p. 20) and Andrea Mantegna. The Palazzo del Tè became, in turn, the model for numerous architectural works north of the Alps, including notably the Palais Waldstein in Prague and the Landshut Residence (p. 88). In 1536, the duke's brother visited Mantua, and from there wrote: 'We had supper in the Palazzo del Tè. As far as I can see, there is no building that has so many exquisite rooms and pictures about which so much could be written and said.'

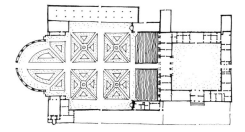

Ground plan

Interior view of the Loggia di Davide

View from the loggia

bottom right:
The façade and main
entrance

PALACE OF CHARLES V
Pedro Machuca

Granada, Spain, 1527–1568

In 1530, Charles V was the mightiest ruler in Europe. As Holy Roman Emperor, he reigned most German-speaking lands and northern Italy, as king of Spain he ruled Castile and Aragon and Spanish America, from where Spain plundered the Caribbean Islands and New Spain (i.e. Mexico). His other realms included Burgundy and the Netherlands, and he exercised influence in Central Europe through his brother Ferdinand, Duke of Austria and King of Bohemia and Hungary.

It was a heterogeneous empire that had no central administration or capital city. Charles V exercised his rule, travelling from place to place, in the tradition of medieval monarchs. Between 1516 and 1544 he spent a quarter of his time on the move. If he had not had his own camp bed, he would have had to sleep in 3,200 different beds. His palace at the Alhambra in Granada, which in any case was intended only as a summer residence, accordingly had a very minor role practically. Documents indicate that Charles V never used it, living instead in the rooms of the Nasrid palace he renovated.

Far more important was the symbolic importance of the palace. Charles V developed the idea with his governor Luis Hurtado de Mendoza, seeing it as a triumphal monument to the Spanish reconquest of Iberia, the Reconquista, which had come to an end on 14 January, 1492, with the capitulation of Boabdil, the last Nasrid sultan of Moorish Granada, to the Catholic Monarchs Isabel of Castile and Ferdinand of Aragon. Granada had until then been in Moorish hands for over 750 years, becoming increasingly important after the Caliphate of Cordoba fell to the Christians in the 13th century. The inscription on the façade of Charles's palace thus reflects the glory he thought due to him: 'SEMPER AUGUSTUS PIUS FELIX INVICTISSIMUS' (for ever emperor, pious, fortunate and invincible).

The architecture of the building completely ignores its Moorish environment and could not be more different from its Nasrid neighbour. The inspiration was Italian – the Palazzo del Tè in Mantua (p. 72) or Raphael's Villa Madama in Rome for the ground plan, and buildings by Bramante for the elevation. Sansovino's Zecca in Venice (p. 80) may also have been a source.

It was also a political avowal by Charles. In 1527, the year work began in Granada, imperial troops had plundered Rome in a military setback for the Pope that has gone down in history as the infamous Sack of Rome. The palace in Granada was intended to celebrate this 'triumph'. Rome was no longer a capital of European art, and Charles V adopted the Pope's traditional position as patron.

In a document dated 1563, the architect of the palace is said to have been Pedro Machuca, although in recent times dissenting voices question whether the Spaniard, who had trained in Rome as a painter, could have acquired the broad cultural and artistic background required to design such an edifice. An alternative name put forward for the design of this unusual palace is Giulio Romano.

Particularly impressive, if otherwise impractical, is the circular inner courtyard, modelled on ancient villa architecture, the designs for the Villa Madama or the house of the painter Andrea Mantegna in Mantua – something that has never been realized in such an idealistic form even in the architecture of subsequent centuries. Later on, bullfights took place here, with the galleries providing room for spectators. The circular court has also been interpreted as Christian symbolism. As early as the 16th century, it served as an allusion to the Virgin's girdle. in any case, during the Renaissance the circle was considered the most perfect of shapes.

Perspective Drawing of the Alhambra, engraving of 1612, from a drawing by Ambrosio de Vico, 1596

Domingo de Velestá, the west front of the Palace of Charles V, engraving from 1793, Academia de San Fernando, Madrid

The east façade of the palace that was never actually lived in by ts builder Charles V

The round, inner courtyard of the palace

CHÂTEAU OF FONTAINEBLEAU
Gilles Le Breton

Fontainebleau, France, begun 1528

On 15 March, 1528, the French king Francis I wrote to the city fathers in Paris: 'I shall in future spend most of my time in Paris. Henceforth I shall conduct my business in this city of God and the area round about.' We may take this letter as the launch of a new artistic policy as well, focusing on the capital. The Loire Valley, where Francis had previously built a château at Chambord (p. 68) and extended another at Blois (p. 64), was now downgraded to the periphery.

Until the Louvre was rebuilt (p. 96), however, the château at Fontainebleau, some 37 miles south-east of Paris, was the real royal residence. Francis's contribution here was the central entrance door (Porte dorée), the following court (Cour ovale), the world-famous Grande Galerie and the new palace (Château Neuf) extending on the west side. As in many other châteaux, the existing structures had to be taken into account and the once residential 15th-century fortified keep, or donjon, is still visible in the corner of the Cour ovale.

Who the architect of the new buildings was we still do not know, though from 1527 Gilles Le Breton is credited as 'General Master of the Royal Building Works'. However, he cannot have been responsible for the Italian features of the architecture such as the Porte dorée, which is reminiscent of the Palazzo Ducale in Urbino (p. 26), or the double-flight staircase in the court, which survived only a few years. Possibly these may be attributed to a certain Pierre Paul, who was known during his lifetime as 'the Italian' and whose tomb makes him the architect of the châteaux of Fontainebleau, Moulins and Bourbon l'Archambault. On the basis of a letter dating from 1528 in which Francis I gives detailed instructions for the new building and which also betrays a certain understanding of architectural matters, Gilles Le Breton has recently been accredited with the design of Fontainebleau.

We can only speculate what Fontainebleau would have looked like if Francis had succeeded in appointing an Italian architect. Instead of Giulio Romano, whom he wanted, he got his pupil Francesco Primaticcio (1505–70), who had collaborated on the interior of the Palazzo del Tè (p. 72), was sent. He and the Florentine painter Rosso Fiorentino (1494–1540) created the Grande Galerie, a type of room that previously existed neither in Italy nor in France. Functionally only a linking corridor within the château, its original feature of windows on both sides and its lavish decoration of inlaid wood, frescoes and opulent stuccowork make the gallery a masterpiece of Renaissance art. The complex subject matter celebrates the person of the king, his character and his rule, almost all of it couched in classical scenes. The style Primaticcio developed would influence French art for decades, and has become known to art history as the School of Fontainebleau. In his *Lives of the Artists,* Giorgio Vasari (cf. p. 112) states that Fontainebleau could claim to be a 'second Rome' – higher praise than that was scarcely conceivable in the 16th century.

The building and its interiors were extended by virtually all later kings until well into the 19th century, the principal additions being a ballroom by Philibert de l'Orme (cf. p. 98), a staircase on the west side and the refurbishment of numerous rooms under Napoleon III.

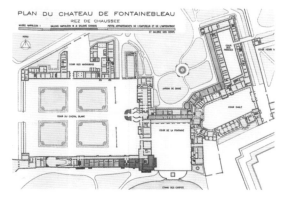

Overall plan of the château

Gilles Le Breton

c. 1500	Born in Paris the son of a traditional stonemason family
1527–	Active in Fontainebleau
1531	Cour ovale
1534	Gardens with water features
1540	Château chapel
1547–	Various houses for aristocrats
c. 1552	Dies in Paris. An inventory of his estate mentions various works of art and nine books on architecture, including Serlio's *Regole generali*

View of the Château of Fontainebleau showing
the Cour du Cheval Blanc

The Grande Galerie

The Porte dorée

GRANADA CATHEDRAL
Diego de Siloé

Andalucia, Spain, 1529–1589

Granada Cathedral is one of the most impressive Renaissance churches in Spain. Its architect, Burgos-born Diego de Siloé, was thoroughly at home in Italian art which put him in a position to create something unique. Only the ground plan of the church is traditionally Spanish and, with its double aisles and ambulatory, is reminiscent of Toledo Cathedral (begun 1226). The elevation possibly takes up the style of Bramante, or the façade of Sant'Andrea in Mantua (p. 28), though many classical buildings may have served as a model.

The foundation stone of the church was laid on 15 March, 1529. Granada had been regained from the Moors in 1492, after which various other buildings had served as an interim cathedral, such as the 'royal' mosque in the Alhambra. A first plan for the new church by the architect and sculptor Enrique de Egas was carried out from the early 1520s only as far as the

Francisco Heylan, *Sectional View of the Cathedral Chancel*, c. 1612

foundations for the outside walls. How Egas came to be replaced by Diego de Siloé still has to be clarified.

In the mid-16th century it was said that Siloé 'continued what Master Enrique had constructed, but in fact he altered it to the Roman style, whereas up to then a modern building had been planned'. At that time, 'modern' meant Gothic, a style Egas had worked in especially in Toledo and in Granada from 1505 in the vault of the Catholic Kings on the south side of the cathedral. Thus, instead of 'modern' Gothic, the style of the church was to be 'Roman', i.e. Renaissance. From our present-day point of view, the term 'modern' would of course have been more appropriate to describe the Renaissance style. In early 16th-century Spain – as of course in many other European countries – the two styles were equally on offer, as it were. When it came to Granada Cathedral, the Renaissance style was chosen, because it allowed for a very particular symbolism. In all probability, the decision can be attributed to Charles I, who was also the Holy Roman Emperor Charles V. In the latter capacity, he saw himself as the successor to rulers of antiquity and wanted to demonstrate this in his architectural works, as he did, for example, in his palace in Granada (p. 74).

The domed chancel of Granada Cathedral, an impressive, steeply proportioned space, suggests mausolea of the Italian Renaissance, the chancel of the church of Santissima Annunziata in Florence or the Trivulzio Chapel in San Nazaro in Milan. Also classical buildings in Rome, such as the burial church of Constantine's wife Helena, could have provided models.

The change from Enrique de Egas to Diego de Siloé was also a decision made by the client, as Siloé, who had previously worked on the east end of Malaga Cathedral, was the only architect in Spain able to work in the Renaissance style at that time. Siloé was also responsible for the stained-glass windows and sculpture in Granada, including the notable Puerta del Perdón.

The west façade (1652–67) of the cathedral designed by Alonso Cano

The interior in all its grandeur

View down the nave towards the choir

PIAZZA SAN MARCO
Jacopo Sansovino

Venice, Italy, begun 1529

On 7 April, 1529, Tuscan-born Jacopo Sansovino was appointed state architect (*proto*) of Venice. Among the duties he acquired was the responsibility for maintaining and looking after St Mark's church and most of the other buildings in the piazza around it. The *proto* was the highest office an architect could aspire to in the Serenissima. For Sansovino, it meant a secure income to the day he died and conferred on him the prestige to seek other lucrative work.

An official residence beside the campanile in the piazza was put at his disposal. The highly appealing assumption is that the architect and sculptor would constantly stand at the window of his house, gazing with distaste at the intolerable conditions out there, imagining grandiose new plans for rebuilding and finally overseeing the building work once it got underway. The piazza was obstructed by stalls selling meat, vegetables and baked goods, there were open latrines, and opposite the Doges' Palace were five inns of ill repute.

Sansovino's first – and probably most momentous – act as regards the functionality of the square was to drive out commerce. In future, the piazza would serve only political and religious functions. This certainly accorded with the recommendation of the leading Italian architectural writers of the 15th century, Filarete and Alberti, that trade and politics be kept apart when designing squares. Similarly, Sansovino's second step should be considered in its historical context in order to appreciate its importance. On the south side, he moved the cen-turies-old building line of the square a little way back from the huge tower of St Mark's. This isolated the tower, which he emphasised by adding an entrance loggetta in 1538–40, and opened up extensive perspectives. From the west end of the piazza, not only St Mark's, but also the Doges' Palace could now be seen.

In 1536, following plans drawn up by Sansovino, work began on constructing the state mint (Zecca) beside the splendid Loggetta (itself enriched in 1560 by Sansovino's sculptures and reliefs). This entrance pavilion served as a lobby for the senators assembled in the Doge's Palace for elections. One year later, work was also underway on the Library of St Mark's alongside it, facing the Doges' Palace. The 'Libreria di San Marco', the façade of which extends to no fewer than twenty-one bays, was considered an architectural masterpiece even by contemporaries.

In his architectural treatise, Andrea Palladio calls it 'fine' and 'good', the 'richest and most ornate building constructed since antiquity'. Not only was the building home to the city's important – and from the first public – library but it also accommodated administrative institutions and an elite school. From that time onwards civic offices were accommodated in the buildings around the square, following the example of forums in Ancient Rome. Sansovino's buildings and St Mark's Square are in no small measure responsible for the 16th century being considered the golden age of Venetian architecture.

Jacopo Sansovino
(Jacopo d'Antonio Tatti)

1486	Baptised on 2 July in the Baptistery in Florence
c. 1502	Pupil of Andrea Sansovino, whose name he assumes
Ab 1505	Studies classical sculpture in Rome
1511–18	Statue of St James for Florence's Cathedral
1518–27	Again in Rome: sculpture entitled *Madonna del Parto* in Sant'Agostino
after 1527	Active in Venice
1538	Work starts on the Palazzo Dolfin
c. 1540	Construction of the Church of San Francesco della Vigna in the Florentine style
1570	Dies in Venice on 27 November

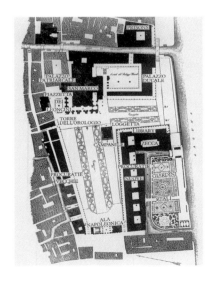

Diagrammatic general view

The façade of Sansovino's library building, the Libreria Vecchia di San Marco

View from the Grand Canal

View of the Libreria, with
the Zecca beyond on the left

The library interior

SAINT-EUSTACHE

Paris, France, begun 1532

On 15 March, 1528, Francis I, king of France, solemnly entered Paris. The date also marks the beginning of the Renaissance in the French capital. Francis ordered the reconstruction of the Louvre, demanded the renovation of the City Hall and introduced a number of urban-planning measures, some of the results of which can still be seen. He had the embankments of the Seine built up and, in the Marais district, work began on the first town houses for the aristocracy.

The most momentous Renaissance church building in France was that of the parish church of Les Halles, next to the city's former central markets. Here Francis I envisaged a grandiose new building, and is supposed to have contributed a substantial amount of his own money to it.

The building history of the church, whose foundation stone was laid in 1532, is rather complex. The first part erected was the south transept, to which nave and choir were then added. The north transept was not finished for another century. Shortly thereafter the façade was deemed to be in a bad way, and the church workshop spent over some thirty years (1754–88) building a new one. Despite the lengthy gestation, the entire work was built to a uniform plan. The architect may have been Dominique de Cortone, though other names mentioned in this connection are Jean Delamarre or Pierre Lemercier, both of whom had previously worked at Saint-Maclou in Pontoise.

The dimensions of the church are huge. In length and breadth, they are almost on the scale of Notre-Dame, whereas the height of the vault in Saint-Eustache surpasses the latter. The new church was much admired in the 17th century, especially for the quantity and variety of the sculptural decoration, the number of piers and chapels, the height of the vaulting and finally the immense extent and variety of the structure as a whole. It was only in the 19th and early 20th centuries that a more analytical eye was cast over its specific combination of Gothic and Renaissance forms. A 1910 description reads: 'Overall, Saint-Eustache is a church with a Gothic-type vault decorated with Renaissance detail. It has the daring and majesty of the great cathedrals of the Middle Ages but the imaginativeness, charm and elegance of sculptural ornament of 16th-century secular buildings. One cannot imagine a lovelier or more splendid church.'

In fact, the double-aisle ground plan right through to the ambulatory derives from Notre-Dame, and the proportions, for example the high, narrow nave, are Gothic. The decorations meanwhile are Renaissance, reflecting contemporary aesthetic tastes. The internal elevation is organised on the same classical sequence of orders as that on the façade of the Palazzo Rucellai in Florence (p. 20), rising from the Doric via the Ionic to the Corinthian order at the top.

Why an exclusively Renaissance-style building was not erected may be due to two reasons: firstly, churches as a whole were conservative structures with firmly established building types that survived for centuries; secondly, Notre-Dame may have been as influential as it was because it was closely associated with the French monarchy. This was the tradition Francis was drawing on as the chief promoter of Saint-Eustache.

Charles Heath, *View of the West Façade of Saint-Eustache*, 1833, after an engraving by Augustus Pugin

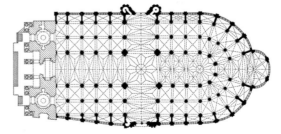

Ground plan

Dominating the former market quarter in Paris: view of the south side of Saint-Eustache from the Forum des Halles

The impressive nave looking to the west

View of the vaulted ceiling

HARTENFELS PALACE
Konrad Krebs

Torgau, Germany, begun 1533

Torgau is on the left bank of the Elbe, 30 miles north of Leipzig, at the crossroads of important ancient trade routes. In the late 15th and especially early 16th centuries the town acquired particular importance as a Saxon royal residence, as the ruling Wettin family came here twice a year to stay in Hartenfels. In 1423, the Wettins had managed to become electors, thereby joining the elite group of German rulers who voted in the Holy Roman Emperor. Thanks to their control of silver mines in the Erzgebirge, they were also fabulously rich.

Hartenfels became famous for its monumental exterior stair tower and the chapel behind it. The latter was one of the first Protestant houses of worship in Germany and, with its two-storey gallery, it is at the same time the only large part of the castle interior to survive in anything like its original state. At its consecration on 5 October, 1544, Martin Luther was the preacher, and he said: 'Wherever the Word of God goes, there God is surely also resident; and again, where the Word is not, there he is not resident, though we may build him a house ever so large.' Unlike in medieval churches, the sermon was heard seated.

Torgau set a pattern. Henceforth, Protestant churches would have chairs or benches facing the pulpit, thus making it easier for the congregation to focus on the services and sermons. The distribution of the seating reflected the social hierarchy of the congregation. Below were ordinary folk, while in the galleries sat the ruling family, divided by sex. The Elector Frederick the Meek had the position of honour on the west side facing the altar. Thus the design and layout of Torgau became a model for many German palace chapels in the 16th century.

The central stair tower also became celebrated, in that it was copied, for example, in the former stair tower in Berlin's city palace. It projects far into the courtyard, an open spiral standing on a tall plinth. In the centre is a hollow newel anchored in the ground, which you can look through from the top as through a funnel. At the top was a private retreat for the elector, where he had an unobstructed view of the landscape. A complicated system of mirrors brought the world into the room. According to a description of 1587, he could see pictures of 'what was happening in the courtyard or the street, or in the country, or what boats were going up and down the River Elbe, or what was happening outside the rooms and inside them.'

Ultimately derived from Blois (p. 64), the stair tower was not just an architectural marvel. Its design and decoration also had their political aspects. The heraldry of Wettin ancestors illustrated the ancient line of the ruling house, while statues of the most important Protestants showed that the new religion was a matter of state. The French connection reflects the political alliance between the Saxon elector and the French king against the Habsburg emperor Charles V. Thus Torgau in its small way reflected major international matters of the day.

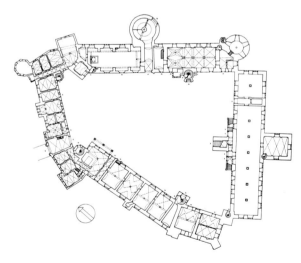

Ground-floor plan, reconstruction of the castle around 1620

Konrad Krebs

c. 1491	Born in 1491 or 1492
1518	Employed on the construction of St Moritz's church in Coburg
1532	On 1 December, appointed architect to Elector John Frederick of Saxony
1537	Travels to Berlin. Employed on the construction of the Stadtschloss
1538–	Active as an architect in Gotha, Eisenach and Wittenberg
1540	Dies on 31 August in Torgau, Germany

General view from the banks of the Elbe

The entrance front

The central stair tower

The interior of the castle chapel

THE OLD REGISTRY (BURGERLIJKE GRIFFIE)
Jan Wallot and Christiaan Sixdeniers

Bruges, Belgium, 1534–1537

From the 13th to the 15th century, the Flemish city of Bruges was one of the most important cities in the Lowlands. Only eight miles from the coast, sea-going vessels could reach it via the Zwin channel, so that trade developed briskly and the city became a prosperous commercial centre. 15th-century travellers described it as a 'large, fine city, rich from its commercial activities' or emphasised the 'excellent houses and streets' and the 'very fine churches and monasteries and superb inns'. When Albrecht Dürer visited the town, he was impressed by the numerous paintings by Hugo van der Goes and Jan van Eyck, also by Michelangelo's Madonna and Child, which is still in the Church of Our Lady. Thanks to Bruges-based painters such as Hans Memling and Gerard David (15th century) and Lancelot Blondeel and Pieter Pourbus (16th century), Bruges became a centre of art. However, as its artistic importance grew in the late 15th century, its commercial importance declined as the Zwin silted up and Antwerp took over its role as the leading commercial port in the Netherlands.

Originally the city was surrounded by a wall no less than five miles long. There were two focal points in the city – the market and the castle of the counts of Flanders. As the Middle Ages drew to a close, the latter fell into disrepair and, from 1434 onwards, served the citizens as a source of building stone. Between the 15th and 18th centuries, the principal public buildings were erected around the site. They included the substantial Brugse Vrije (the former treasure house of the palace) with the Emperor Charles fireplace in the Court Room, containing one of the earliest masterpieces of Renaissance sculpture in the Netherlands, by Blondeel and his assistants *c.* 1529, the Town Hall (built 1376–1420) and the Burgerlijke Griffie.

The latter, a five-bay house constructed by the municipal builder Christaan Sixdeniers to plans by the stone mason Jan Wallot, is a typical example of the early Flemish Renaissance style. Gothic features are combined with classical motifs to form a harmonious whole. The front is dominated by huge windows and the engaged columns framing it at the side. The two uppermost columns have barley-sugar shafts, a feature associated with the entrance to the Temple of Solomon in Jerusalem. At the top are sculptural figures, personifications of the virtues on each side of Moses, Justice and Aaron. Together they constitute emblems of good government. The decoration programme of this elegant building in Bruges thus anticipates that of the Town Hall in Antwerp (p. 116). The building underwent considerable restoration in the late 19th century.

J.-B. van Meunincxhove, *The Market Square in Bruges,* 1701, showing, from *l.* to *r.*: the Provinciaal Museum, the Griffie and Brugse Vrije and the Town Hall

View of the Griffie and Brugse
Vrije from the market square

Detail of rear façade

LANDSHUT RESIDENCE
Giulio Romano (attrib.)

Landshut, Germany, begun after 1536

On 2 March, 1536, the Bavarian duke Louis X (1495–1545) ordered the demolition of four houses to make room for his new city palace. The date marks the commencement of construction work on one of the most modern and, in terms of its interior furnishings, most opulent palaces in Europe. In his own words, Louis wanted to build a 'splendid, handsome building'.

Hitherto the duke had lived in Trausnitz Castle which is perched atop a rocky escarpment overlooking Landshut. This was renovated during his reign – for example, new vaulting was erected in the chapel in 1517/18, and a richly decorated cast-iron oven was ordered in 1529. Why Louis now desired a new, grandiose palace in the centre of town opposite the Town Hall has never been fully explained, but the likely reason is that by the Renaissance period many rulers' castles had lost their defensive *raison d'être* (pp. 40, 64). As Niccolò Machiavelli wrote in his momentous work *The Prince* (1513), 'rulers who are more afraid of their own people than foreign powers should live in fortresses; but those who fear foreign powers more than their own people should refrain from this.' Even in terms of the historical context, a memorable new palace offered Louis X a good way to assert his position among his peers, because politically he was rather at a disadvantage compared with the Wittelsbach branch in Munich.

The new palace occupied a position along the principal street of the town, facing west towards the River Isar. Work began with the narrow four-storey wing facing the street. In its ground plan, it probably followed that of the Fugger houses in Augsburg. The architect, the stonemason and Bernhard Zwitzel, who supervised construction, likewise came from there. Even at this early stage, this part of the palace was called the German Building.

Before the footings were completed and the foundation stone laid on 6 May, 1536, a radical change in the direction of the project had been made. On a visit to Italy, Louis had seen the Palazzo del Tè in Mantua (p. 72), built shortly before by his cousin Federigo Gonzaga. So impressed was Louis by this palace that he immediately wanted his own residence to be built along similar lines, in the Italian style.

Thus between 1537 and 1543 three more wings were built, and the result was an edifice called the Italian Building, even by contemporaries. The supervisor Louis employed was one Master Sigmund, but the design probably came from no less an architect than Giulio Romano. Though documentary proof of this is lacking, the correlations with the Palazzo del Tè and the high architectural quality of the Landshut Residence make his authorship at least probable. Moreover, stuccoworkers were summoned from Mantua to decorate the interior of the palace in a classical style that in the first half of the century was scarcely known north of the Alps.

Virtually all the rooms were splendidly furnished, but particularly the Great Hall and the chapel. Still extant are rich ornamental decoration, fireplaces, inlaid doors and marble floors. The most important part of the original painting work to survive is the altarpiece in the chapel, painted around 1540 by Herman Posthumus – an artist whose importance has been recognised only very recently.

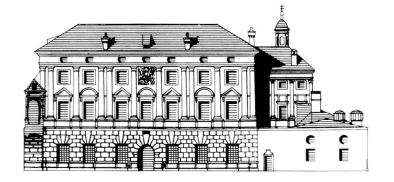

The west façade (the Italian Building)

Giulio Romano
(Giulio di Pietro de' Gianuzzi)

c. 1499	Born in Rome
1509–17	Collaboration with members of Raphael's workshop on the Stanze de Raffaello in the Vatican
1520	Following Raphael's death, pursues various projects, including the interior of the Villa Madama, Rome
c. 1522	Palazzo Maccarani, Rome
c. 1522	Altar painting for Santa Maria dell'Anima, Rome, commissioned by Jakob Fugger
1524	First commission for Federico Gonzaga
1536–38	Interior of the Palazzo Ducale, Mantua
1546	Dies on 1 November

The Italian Room on the first floor the Residence in Landshut. The decorative pilasters date from the 18th century.

The inner courtyard of the Italian Building

Part of the arcades in the inner courtyard

The Italian Building

THE CAPITOL
Michelangelo Buonarroti

Rome, Italy, begun 1537

In antiquity, the Capitol was considered one of the seven wonders of the world, a visible expression of Rome's importance as the *caput mundi* (head of the world). Here stood the hut in which, according to legend, Romulus and Remus had been brought up, here were the temples of the principal Roman gods. State laws and treaties were stored in a building facing the Forum Romanum; and finally in the middle of the site was the holy place of the Asylum, a refuge for exiles. The latter function, which is the source of our present concept of asylum, was still known of in the 16th century. In 1554, the writer and architect Andrea Palladio wrote: 'In the piazza of the Capitol, where the statue of Marcus Aurelius now stands, there was a place called Asylum. It was established by Romulus, to draw all persons to his new city.'

Unlike in the present arrangement, the Capitol, which is on the smallest of Rome's seven hills, was originally orientated to the ancient Forum and accessible only from there. It must have been a huge task for Michelangelo to turn what, by the Middle Ages had become an unprepossessing area called Monte Caprino (Goat Hill), into a majestic focal point again.

A harbinger of things to come was Pope Paul III's decision in 1537 to move the ancient equestrian statue of Emperor Marcus Aurelius from its original position in front of the Lateran to the new square, where Michelangelo installed it on a new plinth in January 1538. It was the starting point for his design of the square.

The alignments and walls of two existing medieval structures had to be respected as points of reference – on the eastern side,

the Palazzo Senatorio, home of the city senate, on the southern side the Palazzo dei Conservatori, where the keepers of Roman antiquities and the city's art collections were accommodated. From the very start of planning, Michelangelo had a reflection of the Palazzo dei Conservatori in mind, combined with a geometric pavement designed by him, but executed as late as the 20th century, thereby creating a unified ensemble. The inspiration for the layout was the 15th-century design for the centre of Pienza (p. 24).

The architecture of the Palazzo dei Conservatori, on the other hand, has no antecedent, even in classical architecture. Pilasters rise through two storeys, a feature that always confers monumentality on a façade. This innovation of Michelangelo's is known as the Colossal, or Giant Order and would become a basic element in the classical grammar of the modern era.

The equestrian statue of Marcus Aurelius has been called the gravitational centre of the Capitol. For many people, the oval surrounding it, which is filled with a twelve-pointed star, furnishes the key to understanding the square. It has been interpreted as an image of the firmament or as an allusion to the twelve apostles. Others would prefer to see the Capitol merely as purely a work of art, devoid of symbolic content. The most fascinating and at the same time historically most conclusive explanation sees the square as a reconstruction of the ancient legal concept of the Asylum, observation of which is guaranteed by the ruler in the middle. In any event, the Capitol is among the most outstanding planning and architectural achievements of the 16th century.

Etienne Dupérac, ground plan of the Capitol, engraving of 1567

Michelangelo Buonarotti

1475	Presumably born on 6 March in Caprese, Tuscany
c. 1487	First sculptural work – a stone relief of the battle of the Centaurs (Casa Buonarroti, Florence)
1488	Trains as a painter in the studio of Domenico Ghirlandaio
after 1501	Statue of David for the Piazza Signoria in Florence
1505	Tomb for Pope Julius II
1508	Paints Sistine Chapel in Rome
1563	Converts the Thermae of Diocletian in Rome into a church
1564	Dies on 18 February in Rome

The steps up to the Capitol with a view of the
Palazzo Senatorio

The inner courtyard of the Palazzo
dei Conservatori

The Piazza del Campidoglio

Now located in the Capitol
Museum: the equestrian
statue of Emperor Marcus
Aurelius

THE BELVEDERE
Paolo della Stella / Bonifaz Wolmut

Hradčany, Prague, Czech Republic, 1538–1563

Although the Bohemian king Ferdinand I lived mainly in Vienna as the Archduke of Austria, he devoted as much, or perhaps even more, attention to the castle in Prague as to the buildings in his inherited territories. He had the law chamber and rooms adjacent to the Vladislav Hall built (p. 40), and commissioned an organ choir for the Cathedral of St Vitus.

However, his most important commissions were the layout of the Royal Garden and the construction of the buildings in it. The extensive park included the Real Tennis Court and the famous villa called, from the 19th century onwards, the Belvedere. The gardens were laid out on the north side of the Hradčany, outside the castle walls, for there was insufficient room for them inside them. Ferdinand summoned gardeners from Italy, Flanders, Spain and Alsace. They created separate sections on the elongated, gently sloping terrain and castle moat – a botanical garden, a herb garden and a *giardinetto* with exotic, ornamental plants. Oranges, lemons, figs and pomegranate trees were introduced and this is where botanist Pier Andrea Matthioli (1501–77) grew Europe's first tulips.

Laid out in 1534, the garden was orientated to the east, and the Belvedere (begun 1538) was constructed at the end, at right angles to the longitudinal axis. Although the villa, considered by many the finest example of Renaissance architecture north of the Alps, was erected in three separate design phases, it looks all of a piece. Around the core of the building on the ground floor is a row of delicate, elegant arches reminiscent of Filippo Brunelleschi's Foundlings' Hospital in Florence (p. 14). They carry a platform, a *bel vedere*, or place to view the fortifications of the castle, the Romanesque Church of St George, the choir of the cathedral and the steep, tree-covered Stag Moat. On top of the second storey of the building, whose sequence of apertures and niches – and indeed overall appearance – recalls that of Bramante's Tempietto in Rome (p. 42), is the curvilinear copper roof, which provides a perfect finish to the Belvedere. The interior, drastically rebuilt in the 19th century, originally had residential quarters on the ground floor, with a huge ballroom above.

The time it took to build (until 1563) was due not just to two changes of architect but more especially to the extensive earthmoving work that the sloping site on the eastern side rendered necessary. The first architect was the Genovese Paolo della Stella, who drew up plans while still in Italy and began work a year later with a team of thirteen Italian stonemasons. Under his guidance, the ground floor and most of the sculptural work were completed, including the stone reliefs which depict mainly mythological scenes.

However, the most important contribution came from the court architect Bonifaz Wolmut, who was responsible for almost all of Ferdinand's projects in Prague. Though trained as a mason, he was a very cultured man, as the surviving part of his library bears out. He even went so far as to have the most important technical books of his day translated into German at his own expense. Among these were Sebastiano Serlio's treatise *L'Architettura*, first published in instalments from 1537 to 1575 (cf. p. 94). Serlio's designs for the door and window surrounds were adapted for the Belvedere.

View of the Belvedere from the garden

Looking along the arcade

CHÂTEAU OF ANCY-LE-FRANC
Sebastiano Serlio

Ancy-le-Franc, France, begun c. 1541

The château of Ancy-le-Franc lies on a plain in Burgundy southeast of Tonnerre. The builder was Comte Antoine III de Clermont-Tonnerre, brother-in-law of Diane de Poitiers, the celebrated mistress of the Valois king Henry II, son of Francis I. The family had been highly regarded ever since it had wisely sided with the Burgundian-born Pope Callistus II in the investiture dispute in the early 12th century. By the mid-16th century, it had become very wealthy, and the count decided he needed a new château. The architect he appointed was the Roman architect Sebastiano Serlio, whom Francis I had summoned to France and appointed royal painter and architect. Serlio's six-part treatise *L'Architettura*, published in instalments from 1537 to 1575, made him the most influential Italian architect in France – to secure his services conferred prestige on the client as well. Around this time, Serlio was also at work on an *hôtel* (town house) for the Cardinal of Ferrara in Fontainebleau (now almost completely destroyed), and this with Ancy-le-Franc would set a long-term model for French architecture in terms of layout and style.

A comparison with Pierre Lescot's Louvre (p. 96) shows how the Italian style of architecture differed from the French in the mid-16th century. In particular, Serlio completely abandoned all sculptural decoration, and designed façades in which the proportions stressed the horizontal rather than the vertical axis. At Ancy-le-Franc, the sole progression from the outside to the inside is the greater profusion of architectural detail. The exterior does not reveal the internal room arrangement.

Instead, the château introduces a wholly new feature to French architecture in the form of four equally long and impressive wings that meet at the corners to create a quadrangle. The corners are accentuated by strongly projecting pavilions that are one storey higher than the wings and are surmounted by pyramidal roofs. Originally there were small lanterns on top of these, but later building work permanently altered the appearance of Ancy-le-Franc.

To gain an idea of the original design, contemporary drawings need to be studied, especially – as for many other buildings – *Les Plus excellents Bastiments de France* that Jacques Androuet du Cerceau the Elder (before 1520 – c. 86) published from 1576 to 1579. Cerceau made engravings of thirty royal and noble castles and châteaux, ranging from the medieval to the contemporary, presenting the general public with views of each accompanied by a short text. The drawing of Ancy-le-Franc also shows the large garden originally planted and the different access arrangements – in the 16th century, the château was completely surrounded by a moat that could only be crossed at two points. The earth and stones removed when the moat was dug were used to create a terrace which encircled the entire building. The original appearance of the château must have been considerably more impressive.

Sebastiano Serlio

1475	Born the son of a furrier, on 6 September in Bologna
c. 1514	Active in Rome, following training as a painter
c. 1537/50	Compiles his treatise *L'Architettura*, which is published in instalments
1541	Travels to the court of Francis I in France
1541/43	Grotte des Pins in Fontainebleau
1547	Following the death of Francis I, is replaced by Philibert de l'Orme as court architect
c. 1553/55	Dies, presumably in Fortainebleau

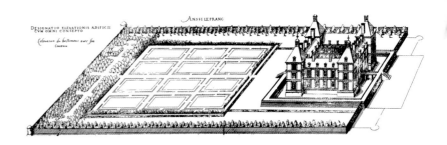

Jacques Androuet du Cerceau, view of the château and its park, from *Les plus excellents Bastiments de France*, c. 1546

View of the entrance front

The inner courtyard

The Medea Gallery

The Salle des Gardes

THE LOUVRE
Pierre Lescot

Paris, France, begun 1546

These days, the Louvre is visited mainly for the works of art on display there, which have turned the former royal castle and palace into one of the most important museums in the world. But the building itself is also notable, the most recent addition being the glass pyramid at the entrance (1983–87) designed by Ieoh Ming Pei in the huge Cour Napoléon.

The planning and building history goes back to the Middle Ages, making the Louvre one of the most interesting locations in French architectural history. Of the earliest building (c. 1200) all that remains are the wall foundations of a mighty bastion built by the Capetian king Philip Augustus (Philip II) north of the Seine, at the strategically critical point where, at that time, the river entered the city. This was the core of the present Louvre. In the 14th century, the Valois king Charles V ('The Wise') turned the Louvre into a castle, the most important internal feature of which was a *grand vis*, or spiral staircase, that would inspire a later generation of château architects (e.g. at Chambord; p. 68).

Then, on 15 March, 1528, Francis I announced his intention to live permanently in Paris and in this connection to rebuild the Louvre. However, it was not until 1546, the year before his death, that work actually began. Francis's successor Henry II adhered to his father's plans more or less faithfully, only a staircase being moved to accommodate a larger ballroom. By 1563, a building had been completed that was architecture – as was said a few years later – 'of such outstanding symmetry and beauty that another work of this kind is scarce to be found in Europe'.

The architect of this new work was Pierre Lescot. He replaced the old Great Hall of the castle with the eastern part of the Cour Carrée. This is actually only a nine-bay façade, but its elegance and sophistication mark it out as a masterpiece of French Renaissance architecture. The sculptural decoration was done by Rouen-born Jean Goujon (c. 1510–68). The numerous reliefs follow an apparently complex but ultimately quite straightforward thematic programme. The central pavilion is surmounted by a prominent H, the initial of the king who establishes and guarantees peace. In turn, Learning and Prosperity (depicted left and right) can flourish.

The architecture of the Louvre was recently described as an 'absolutely self-assured design by an inspired artist'. Particularly convincing is the clarity of the elevation. Three slightly projecting pavilions (*risalti*) break up the three-storey façade, each enclosing an entrance to the building. The central pavilion is slightly higher and therefore more prominent. Borrowings from Italian architecture are restricted here to individual features, such as columns and window surrounds. The verticality of the façade is utterly different from the Italian style.

The ground floor is occupied by a huge ballroom, which has achieved fame largely because of the gallery carried by four caryatides. These were likewise conceived by Goujon and are near-replicas of the caryatides adorning the Erechtheum on the acropolis in Athens. Thus it was not only Roman antiquity that interested Renaissance architects (cf. p. 9). In the Renaissance work of the Louvre, the staircase with its sculptures, the caryatides and the façade decoration represent a marriage of sculpture and architecture that is both impressive and expressive.

Partial view from the *Plan de Turgot*, 1739

Pierre Lescot

c. 1500/10	Born, probably in Paris. Inherits the title of Seigneur de Clagny
1541–44	Screen of Saint-Germain-l'Auxerrois (destroyed 1750)
1546–78	The Louvre
1546	Hôtel de Ligneris (now Carnavalet) in Paris (attributed)
1549	Fontaine des Innocents on the occasion of Henry II's entry into Paris (attributed). Collaboration with Jean Goujon
1578	Dies on 10 September in Paris

The east wing of the Cour Carrée. The left-hand section dates from 1546–63; the right-hand section, Sully Pavillon and Lemercier Wing from 1624 onwards

The Salle des Cariatides with Jean Gonjon's gallery against the rear wall

The Cour Napoléon looking towards the palace façades erected between 1852 and 1857 with I.M. Pei's glass pyramids in front

CHÂTEAU OF ANET
Philibert de l'Orme

Dreux, France, 1548–1552

The Château at Anet, a small town a few miles north of Dreux, near Chartres in northern France, survives only in part. Remants of the original work include the triumphal entrance gateway and parts of the southern enclosing wall with a side gateway. Of the château itself, only the chapel (consecrated 1577) and the west wing (heavily altered in the 18th century) survive. An early example of deliberate preservation, the frontispiece of the central *corps de logis* was removed to Paris in the late 18th century and can now be seen in the courtyard of the Ecole des Beaux-Arts.

The château was commissioned by one of the 16th century's most memorable women, Diane de Poitiers (1500–66). Widow of an aristocrat and mistress of Henry II, she was highly intelligent and power-conscious, exercising considerable influence on the king's political decisions. She was also a munificent patron of the arts. For her deceased husband, for example, she commissioned a lavish tomb in Rouen Cathedral in 1535, the design and complex subject matter of which make it one of the most notable works of French Renaissance sculpture.

The architect of Anet, Philibert de l'Orme, had to take the walls of a predecessor building into account in his design. Around 1470, Diane de Poitier's husband's grandfather had begun work on a small manor house, which Diane herself extended in 1545–47. De l'Orme's design of 1548 allowed for a three-wing arrangement around a square court, with further quadrangles on each side. In the west was the famous Fountain of Diana (now in the Louvre) depicting the resident of the palace in the guise of the goddess of hunting. On the eastern side, the parts of the old building were neatly integrated into the layout. As an endpiece, the architect built a gate adorned with embrasures and water spouts in the shape of gun barrels. This was an ironic allusion to the earlier function of the manor house as a fortified building.

Anet's exclusive qualities were readily recognised by contemporaries. Along with the usual comments that 'there's nothing like it anywhere', it was bestowed with epithets such as 'paradise' and 'Dianet' – terms that also alluded to the special attraction of its owner.

Architecturally, the outstanding features are the entrance façade of the château and the chapel, a centralised building inspired by Palladio's church in Maser. The gate is an interesting variant of the Roman triumphal arch, though its Mannerist attic storey is de l'Orme's own invention, lending the architecture a sculptural quality. On top is a stag facing the courtyard, surrounded by four hounds. The figures are connected to a clock in which the hours were originally marked by the stag striking its hoof against a bell and the dogs barking. Thus the gate is a mixture of architecture, sculpture and sophisticated mechanisms.

A number of terraces gave a view over the town and the château with its huge garden extending northwards enclosed by colonnades and pavilions. For the first time in French art, cultivated nature was incorporated into an architectural framework.

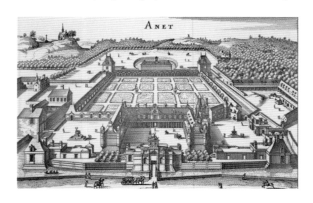

Château of Anet, engraving by Matthäus Merian the Elder, 1655

Philibert de l'Orme

1514	Born in Lyon, probably between 3–9 June
1533–36	Trains as an architect – probably with his father. Travels to Rome
1548	On 7 April, appointed court architect to Henry II
1547/48–58	Tomb of Francis I and his wife in Saint-Denis
c. 1550	Active in Fontainebleau
1563–70	For Catherine de' Medici, worked on several projects, including the Tuileries in Paris (1871 torched during the Commune)
1567	Publishes *Le premier Tome de l'architecture* (The First Book of Architecture), the most important architectural book in 16th-century France
1570	Dies in Paris on 8 January 1570

A true masterpiece of Renaissance architecture: the entrance gateway to the château

The château chapel

The west side-wing

POZNAŃ TOWN HALL
Giovanni Battista Quadro

Poznań, Poland, 1552–1560

The Town Hall in Poznań is first documented in 1310. The medieval building clearly comprised a simple, multi-storey cube with a tower in the north-west corner. Following various additions and a serions fire in 1536, it was rebuilt from 1552 to 1560 so as to constitute virtually a new building, extending east and westwards to double the original size. The most important construction works concerned the main façade facing the market and the great Council Chamber on the first floor.

In contrast to many other Renaissance town halls in Europe (pp. 106, 116, 136), neither the façade nor the Council Chamber was decorated with sculptures or paintings. Only in the spandrels of the arcading on the impressive three-storey loggia to the front are relief figures applied. Inside, the splendid ceiling of the Council Chamber also displays a few figural scenes and other ornamentation. However, no political programme is discernible in these, so Poznan's Town Hall must be appreciated largely for its architectural qualities.

The main façade is the most striking feature. The open loggias are framed by blind arches, which continue above as polygonal turrets. Between the latter is an exceptionally tall attic storey crowned by a sort of battlement, giving the edifice the look of a fortified palace. The architectural detail increases from bottom to top, while diminishing in scale and prominence. The façade thus looks like a framed picture.

The city appointed Lugano-born Giovanni Battista Quadro as the architect of the building in 1552 and, in the same year, he was appointed city architect as well. Remaining in this post for nearly forty years, he designed public buildings and supervised their construction. He brought his three brothers, Antonio, Gabriele and Chiliano and a whole series of assistants with him to Poznań. Between them, they revolutionised the appearance of the city. Quadro's architectural style indicates close familiarity with northern Italian buildings. Once again, the works of Sebastiano Serlio (cf. p. 94) were a major influence, particularly with respect to the original – now considerably altered – entrance steps, a number of doorways and the vaulting of the Council Chamber.

In winter 1945, the Town Hall was largely destroyed in heavy fighting in Poznań. It was reconstructed in the post-war years (until 1954), and restored in recent years. Unlike the previous restorations in 1783, 1913 and 1919, the work was carried out with the utmost care. In earlier restorations, coats of arms and inscriptions had been added and removed depending on whether the city belonged to Poland or Germany.

Detail of the façade

View of the Town Hall from the square

VILLA HVEZDA (STAR VILLA)
Ferdinand II and Hans Tirol

Near Prague, Czech Republic, 1555–1558

Around 1530, Ferdinand I established a large game park just outside Prague and this was used in the 16th century principally for royal hunting parties. Subsequently Ferdinand's son, Archduke Ferdinand II of Tyrol (1529–95), commissioned the construction of a villa in the park under the supervision of a certain Hans Tirol, though the architects who oversaw the construction were Italians, Giovanni Maria Aostalli and Giovanni Lucchese. Then, around 1558, Bonifaz Wolmut, the architect of the Belvedere in Prague (p. 92), added fortifications to it in the Italian style.

The plan for the building came from the archduke himself, to which five signed drawings in his own hand now in the Austrian National Library attest. They indicate how important the planning process had become in architectural history, as well as pro-

Drawing by Ferdinand II of the ground plan of the Villa Hvezda

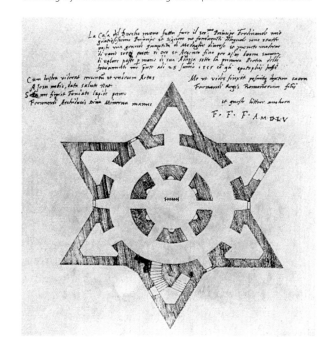

viding a further example of a client acting as his own architect (pp. 10–12). Ferdinand II, who also dabbled in glass-blowing, metal-casting and woodturning, employed 'unimaginative artists so as to teach them what they had to do and make'. The artists could thus be considered merely as vehicles for implementing a client's ideas.

No doubt this accounts for the idiosyncratic design of the building – both the ground plan and elevation with the roof are star-shaped. This is so unusual in architectural history that the 'star' epithet also became the name of the building. The ground plan reveals a twelve-point central area vaulted by a dome, adjoining six narrow barrel-vaulted corridors that lead to rhomboid-shaped rooms. The visitor thus experiences the villa as a labyrinth offering an endless series of surprising spatial experiences. Convenience and functionality were sacrificed to symmetry of ground plan for the purpose of visual effect. One might say the same about Chambord (p. 68) or the Villa Rotonda (p. 120).

However, seen from the outside, the edifice looks straightforward enough – one might even call it austere. There is no main front. The building thus reflects the theoretical ideal of 16th-century sculpture that a work should be beautiful from every angle.

The interior is decorated with stuccowork illustrating Ovid's *Metamorphoses*, conferring stylistic up-to-dateness on the villa. Wall niches in the rhomboid rooms were presumably originally intended to accommodate statues or weaponry. Had this intention been realised, the villa would have been one of the earliest collections of art in the modern era.

The entrance front

Details of the stuccowork in the dome over the central room

LEIPZIG TOWN HALL
Hieronymus Lotter / Paul Speck

Leipzig, Germany, 1556/1557

In 1485, it was said of the Saxon commercial and university city of Leipzig that 'its burghers swim in money. Rich Frankfurt, the old coronation city on the Main, can't keep up.' From late medieval times, the importance of Leipzig had been growing steadily, mainly as a result of the thrice-yearly trade fair and the newly discovered silver mines. The town was becoming one of Germany's principal cities.

The rebuilding of the Town Hall was a clear expression of Leipzig's high faith in itself. The result has sometimes been re-fered to as be one of the finest secular buildings in Europe. At any rate, it was certainly one of the first Renaissance buildings in Germany. For every town, rebuilding its most important communal building was a way of expressing its self-assurance and its power, especially relative to the state. In Leipzig, rebuilding was also a matter of urgent necessity, as the old Town Hall was dilapidated and, as was noted in the mid-16th century, had already 'had to be propped up in many places' by earlier generations.

The brief was to make the new building 'incomparable'. The city was fortunate in having Hieronymus Lotter as builder. Besides being thoroughly versed in Italian and Flemish architecture, Lotter was also a highly successful merchant. His singular status as a 16th-century artist is indicated by the fact he was elected mayor eight times.

Designs for the Town Hall were probably drawn up by the stonemason Paul Speck (cf. p. 10). Lother took charge of construction work, monitored the allocation of funds and the purchase of building materials, and was obviously such an outstanding organiser that the building was completed in the sensationally short time of only ten months.

The Town Hall, a rectangular building occupying the whole east side of the marketplace, lies in the city centre. The arches on the ground floor are a later addition – originally there were simple shops here. The steeply pitched roof is punctuated by six lucarnes of varying size and in the middle there is a tall tower incorporating a staircase. The particular artistic quality lies in the harmonious, balanced proportions of the structure.

Like virtually all town halls, Lotter's building had to serve several functions. Originally the mayor had his office here, and the city council and municipal court held sessions in the rooms on the upper floor. As a special princely favour, Leipzig had become the seat of the Saxon royal supreme court in 1488. In addition, the Town Hall provided space for trade and crafts and the burghers were permitted to make use of the Great Hall for festive occasions.

In the hall and adjacent rooms there are still a number of original furnishings from the 16th century, such as a magnificent cupboard from 1592, and a musicians' gallery reminiscent of a comparable feature in the Louvre (p. 96). In its balanced design and capacious arrangement of rooms, Leipzig Town Hall inspired a whole series of municipal buildings in Saxony and southern Germany.

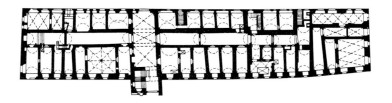

The ground plan before rebuilding, 1906

Hieronymus Lotter

1497	Born in Nuremberg, Germany
1520	Settles in Leipzig. Active entrepreneur in the metal and cloth trades
1548	Appointed architect to Elector John Frederick of Saxony
1555–73	Elected mayor of Leipzig eight times
1568	Principal architect of the Augustusburg on the Schellenberg
1572	Removed from office, with subsequent financial ruin
1580	Dies 24 July in Geyer, where he had settled

Leipzig Town Hall: the prototype for many others throughout Germany

The Town Hall and market in an engraving by Joachim Ernst Schefler, 1749

The musician's gallery (Pfeiferstuhl)

BURGHLEY HOUSE
Sir William Cecil (Lord Burghley)

Stamford, Northamptonshire, England, 1556–1587

Burghley House is one of the largest great houses built in the Elizabethan era. Particularly impressive are the west entrance front and the clock tower in the inner courtyard. The client was the statesman Sir William Cecil (1520–98), who was knighted in 1551 and made a baron in 1571. During Elizabeth I's reign, he was Chief Secretary of State and (from 1572) Lord High Treasurer, thus combining two principal state offices.

Like many prominent English house-builders, he had a lively interest in the architecture of his day. His correspondence indicates that he had read the ten books by the classical architect and writer Vitruvius (*De Architectura*) and was familiar with contemporary Flemish and French architecture. It is therefore quite logical that Burghley House should become one of the few buildings in which the Renaissance style – as understood on the Continent – be reflected in English architecture.

In a letter, Cecil makes specific reference to the French architect Philibert de l'Orme. It is wholly conceivable that Cecil himself was the one who decided that two French sources should be combined in the design of his clock tower – the three-storey elevation reflects the Porte Dorée at Fontainebleau (p. 76) and the pyramidal chapel roof at the Château of Anet (p. 98). Here, as 16th-century books indicate, the pyramid functions as a symbol of immortality and princely fame, an iconography that the cultured client was certainly aware of. With a hands-on approach of this sort, Cecil was acting as a kind of amateur architect whose ideas were put into effect by the mason, John Symonds.

The staircase in the north-west of the building also goes back to French models, such as the staircase in the Louvre (p. 96) erected in Henry II's reign. However, in its ground plan Burghley House followed the model of great English houses and country seats. The elevation also adopts a standard English pattern, such as the original Somerset House in London or – for example, in the outline of the west wing at Hampton Court (p. 62).

The house was erected on a site that had been in the ownership of the Cecil's for a generation. Work began in 1556 with the Great Hall and a huge kitchen, both of which dominate the house's external appearance, rising clearly above the ridges of the nearby roofs. With its rib vaulting, the interior is Gothic. It was only in the 1570s and 1580s that Renaissance motifs began to appear. This new phase in the building history of Burghley House can be linked with the immensely enhanced prestige of the client. The interior of the house was later radically altered and an outstanding feature here is the decoration of the chapel with an altar painting by Paolo Veronese.

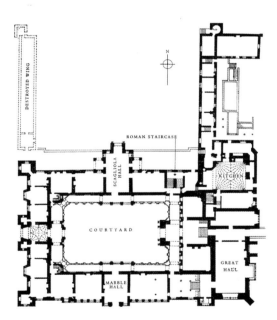

Ground plan

The west front of Burghley House

Interior view of the stair tower

The Great Hall

The inner courtyard with clock tower

ST PETER'S
Michelangelo Buonarroti

Rome, Italy, from c. 1551

After the Church of the Holy Sepulchre in Jerusalem, St Peter's is the most important church in Christendom. The first church, a basilica with double aisles, was built around 320 during the reign of Constantine on the supposed site of St Peter's crucifixion, and over the next millennium or so it became the religious centre of the Western Christian Church. This was also where virtually all popes were buried, as successors to St Peter.

Extensive parts of the Early Christian building survived into the early 17th century, but radical rebuilding was already being considered in Pope Nicholas v's day (1447–55). Partly in disrepair, the church was hardly suited to modern requirements. Altars, tombs and memorials of all kinds filled every nook and cranny, and there had long ceased to be room for the papal household in the apse at the west end. The immense tide of pilgrims found it difficult to reach the tomb of St Peter and during mass the congregation could hardly have seen or heard anything.

Planning for the new building therefore focused on the west end, where suitable provision was needed for the high altar, the papal throne and St Peter's tomb. The history of the project, from the initial Greek cross design by Donato Bramante and its continuation by Michelangelo through to Carlo Maderno's addition of a nave from 1607, could be described as a chain of innovations, though an alternative reading would tell of the gradual destruction of the venerable Old St Peter's.

Even at planning stage, the new building elicited superlatives. It was said to surpass the most famous sanctuaries of antiquity in size, or was like the Pantheon rolled in with the Basilica of Maxentius. Like many other buildings, St Peter's was also rated as one of the wonders of the world, which were multiplying rather quickly at this time (pp. 68, 116).

Criticism was equally uninhibited. Rumour had it that the legendary indulgences for the New St Peter's, supposedly freeing purchasers of sin while paying for bricks and mortar, were in fact being used by the pope to finance his sister's lifestyle. The new church was thus a major contributory factor to the Reformation.

Construction work was carried out in several phases: after a tentative start in the 15th century, real work began to Bramante's design in 1506 under Pope Julius ii, until brought to a stop by the architect's death in 1514. Construction resumed in 1547, when Paul iii appointed the seventy-two-year-old Michelangelo as architect. In a celebrated polemic of 1546, Michelangelo had dismissed the argument that had raged since Bramante's death, criticising all the proposals for numerous subsidiary rooms as 'offering dark hidey-holes that would tempt people to countless crimes such as concealing wanted criminals, forging false coin and impregnating nuns'.

By the time of Michelangelo's death in 1564, a major part of the building had been completed under his supervision. St Peter's was by then well on its way to becoming a true architectural wonder. It was left to Bernini to complete the magic we know today with his Baroque sense of the theatrical, notably the tabernacle, papal throne and colonnaded piazza.

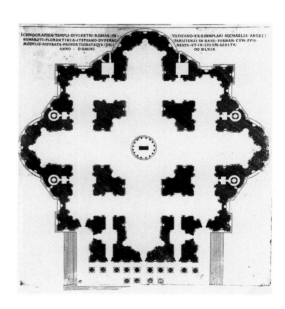

Etienne Dupérac, ground plan of St Peter's in Rome based on Michelangelo's design, engraving of 1569

View from St Peter's Square. The façade was completed to a design by Carlo Maderno between 1607 and 1612

Looking down the nave towards the west

View up into the dome

PALAZZO FARNESE
Giacomo Vignola

Caprarola, near Rome, Italy, 1559–1573

The noted French essayist Michel de Montaigne wrote of his visit to the villa at Caprarola in 1581: 'This building is surrounded by a deep moat hewn out of the tufa; it is pentagonal in form but looks like a pure rectangle. Inside, however, it is perfectly round.' Montaigne was relating his first impression, one that is still experienced by visitors to the little town 34 miles northwest of Rome. The main street of the town rises up a steep slope, while the imposing structure of the villa is set back behind a forecourt and initially all you see is a rectangle. The entrance to the building is eclipsed almost entirely by huge corner bastions. This leaves one quite unprepared as one enters the interior courtyard which, like that of the Palace of Charles v in Granada (p. 74), is completely round. Montaigne described its geometric shape quite soberly. Clearly it is only in our time that adequate words can be found to convey the heady impression of the architecture. Montaigne wrote: 'the sphere of hermetic unity … in which the viewer of architecture is granted the rather rare experience [invokes] complete disorientation.'

With the interplay of round and angular shapes at the Palazzo Farnese, Giacomo Vignola displays a virtuosity that is rare in architectural history. Indeed, it is only possible to appreciate fully the architectural sleights of hand he uses through isometric projections. These provide a ground plan, elevation and section through the building and demonstrate, for example, how the rectangular entrance area provides access to the interior court as well as to a spiral staircase and a circular chapel on the opposite side. Dynamism seems to be the guiding principle. The result for the visitor is that it is an exciting experience to approach and explore the building.

The pentagon was not Vignola's idea, but the round interior was. Work had begun on the foundation walls by Antonio da Sangallo the Younger and Baldassare Peruzzi in the early 1520s, and was resumed as late as 1559. Vignola also built a palace for his client, the Farnese family, in Piacenza and the church of Il Gesù in Rome (p. 124). By the end of the 16th century, the interior of the Palazzo Farnese was adorned by the brothers Taddeo and Federico Zuccaro with elaborate frescoes, which are among some of the finest of the period.

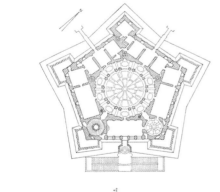

Ground plan

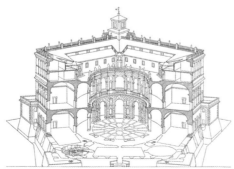

Section drawing,
from an engraving by
Giovanni Battista Falda

Giacomo Vignola
(Giacomo Barozzi da Vignola)

1507	Born on 1 October in Vignola, the son of an artist family
1541	Appointed architect of the basilica of San Petronio in Bologna
1541–43	Involved in making copies of classical sculptures for Fontainebleau
1545	Work starts on the Palazzo Bocchi in Bologna
1449	Commissions from the pope: Villa Giulia, Rome; Sant'Andrea in Via Flaminia
1550	Commissions from the Farnese family
1562	*La Regola delli Cinque Ordini d'Architettura* (The Rule for the Five Orders of Architecture), most important architectural textbook until the 19th century
1573	Dies on 7 July in Rome

View of the entrance front facing the town

View up the stairwell to the ceiling

Detail of the stairs

The colonnade in the
round inner courtyard

THE UFFIZI
Giorgio Vasari

Florence, Italy, begun 1559

The Uffizi building is the most impressive structure constructed in cinquecento Florence. Originally it housed offices (*uffizi*) of the principal ministries and officials of the republic-turned-grand duchy. Only from the 1580s onwards was it gradually transformed into the world-famous museum now associated with the name. In 1581, shortly after the Uffizi were completed, the columned hall upstairs was closed, the walls were frescoed and classical statues were installed. In 1584, Bernardo Buontalenti created one of the first museum displays of modern times, in the octagonal room called the Tribuna, which was hung with the most important paintings of the Medici collection.

Vasari had initially planned a long, four-winged arrangement with a mausoleum for Cosimo I, Duke of Tuscany in the middle. As implemented, the Uffizi were far more original, forming a continuous street front occupying the space between the city's principal government building – the Palazzo della Signoria – and the bank of the Arno. The result was a triumphal way flanked by grand façades with a vista one way towards the Piazza della Signoria, the other way towards the river, as in a work of central perspective. Vasari's design thus also set new standards in terms of urban planning.

Unlike for villas, churches and palaces, there were no prototypes for administrative buildings, as previous to the 16th century this kind of building simply did not exist. In the event, Vasari looked for inspiration to arrangements such as San Marco in Venice (p. 80). For the individual features of the architecture, inspiration was drawn mainly from works by Michelangelo, such as the Biblioteca Laurenziana, also in Florence (p. 70). The result was that an architectural idiom originally developed for the interior of a building was transferred to a façade. Consequently, the space lined by these façades took on the character of an inner courtyard.

Originally a dozen or so different institutions were housed in the Uffizi. They included various large guilds and some smaller ones, the court of commerce, various government officials and the state archives. Each had to pay for its own office to be built, so that a large part of the overall building costs were covered by the sum of individual contributions. Each of the institutions had a separate entrance from the barrel-vaulted ground floor, the wooden doors of which – those that survive, at least – still carry the original names of the offices. The various institutions thus shared a single, unifying façade.

The Uffizi are Vasari's most notable architectural work, though he is better known for his famous *Lives of the Artists*. When his numerous paintings are also taken into account, his claim to be a universal man is evident. His œuvre is another clear indication of the supremacy Florence had achieved by the mid-16th century. On a political level, long-standing rival Siena had been vanquished in 1555, and in 1569 Cosimo I finally became the first Grand Duke of Tuscany.

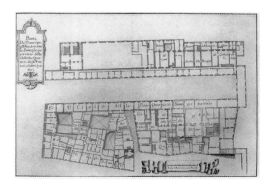

Giuseppe Ruggieri, ground plan of the palace complex, 18th century

Giorgio Vasari

1511	Born on 30 July in Arezzo
1532	First surviving work, a picture of the Burial of Christ (Casa Vasari, Arezzo). Had previously trained as a painter and goldsmith
1546	Takes only 100 days to paint a room in the Palazzo della Cancelleria
1550	First edition of *Lives of the Artists*, the most important biographical work of Renaissance art
1555–72	Refurbishes the Palazzo Vecchio, Florence
1574	Dies in Florence on 27 June

The south façade along the banks of the Arno

left: Interior view of the east corridor with its 16th-century frescos

below left: View through the inner courtyard towards the river

below: the Sala dei Tribuni; one of the first museum rooms of the modern era

PALAZZO PITTI
Bartolomeo Ammannati

Florence, Italy, 1560–1578

The Palazzo Pitti is named after the man who had it built, Luca Pitti. The seven bays in the middle, which still form the core of the façade, were constructed from 1457 to 1461. The design is based on that of the Palazzo Medici (p. 16), but surpassed the latter in scale. A 17th-century anecdote describes this comparison as rivalry between Cosimo de' Medici and Luca Pitti. According to the story, Pitti wanted the windows of his palace to be larger than those in the doorways of the Palazzo Medici.

In terms of urban landscape, the Palazzo Pitti also provides a notable feature in that it is set back from the line of the ancient Via Romana by more than 50 yards, leaving ample room for a spacious forecourt commensurate with the width of the façade. At the side are two lower rows of buildings. Although in the 15th century these were not yet incorporated into the palace as wings of a unified whole, the arrangement nonetheless anticipated the *cour d'honneur* with which the Palazzo Pitti – as the seat of the Medici dynasty – would be graced in the following centuries.

From 1560 to 1578, Bartolomeo Ammannati constructed his famous interior courtyard, while from the beginning of the 17th century until 1839 successive extensions to the façade brought the total width to its present twenty-five windows. As with the Palazzo Medici, the older building was preserved, but adapted in design and interior decoration to new requirements.

As first built, the palazzo had no inner courtyard, work having stopped in 1469 after Pitti got hopelessly into debt. He wrote to the tax authorities in that year: 'As I have already indicated, I have been building, and in the meantime the costs of this have doubled, such that I have had to ask for money from relatives,

friends, merchants and artists. And I have run up substantial debts about which I wish to give no details, so as not to injure those who have served me.'

The new interior courtyard, begun in February 1562, borrows motifs from the façade to make a three-wing layout featuring rusticated columns. Around the same time, Andrea Palladio was using a similar approach for the Villa Sarego near Verona. The huge working blocks came incidentally from a quarry in the grounds of the palazzo. They were probably the largest ever used since antiquity.

The best view of the interior courtyard is from the Bóboli Gardens, a huge area of over a hundred acres laid out from 1550 by sculptors Niccolò Tribolo and Giambologna and architects Giorgio Vasari, Bernardo Buontalenti and Ammannati himself. A fantastic grotto, a hippodrome and an open-air theatre, fountains and water features along with sculptural groups offered a calculated series of surprises for the senses.

The impresario behind the programme was the new tenant of the palazzo, Duke Cosimo I de' Medici. With the rebuilding of the old governmental building of Florence, the Palazzo Vecchio, the construction of the Uffizi (p. 112) and the extension of the Palazzo Pitti, he restored Florence to the forefront of artistic development in Italy. The architect of the Uffizi, Vasari, built him a private walkway linking all the buildings, now known as the Corridoio, at first-floor level. This allowed the duke to walk through the city unseen, even across the Ponte Vecchio over the River Arno. The Corridoio's small windows meant that the populace could be watched by the duke at any time without anyone being aware.

Bartolomeo Ammannati

1511	Born on 18 June in Settignano near Florence
c. 1523–27	Trains as a sculptor in the studio of Baccio Bandinelli
1557–74	Palazzo Grifoni, Florence
1558–59	Constructs vestibule stair of the Biblioteca Laurenziana to plans by Michelangelo
c. 1560–75	Fountain of Neptune in the Piazza della Signoria, Florence
1567–70	Bridge of Santa Trinità, Florence
1592	Dies in Florence on 13 April

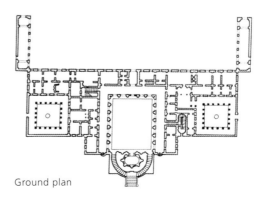

Ground plan

The property of the state since 1919 and now the home to museums and galleries: the Palazzo Pitti viewed from the Via Romana

The inner courtyard showing the so-called 'rustic' stonemasonry

The Sala dell'Iliade with its decorative programme which comes from the early 19th century

ANTWERP TOWN HALL
Cornelis Floris

Antwerp, Belgium, 1561–1565

Antwerp's Town Hall is the most important Renaissance build-ing in the Netherlands, which in the 16th century belonged to Spain. With its impressive façade it was a visible expression of the immensely increased prestige of the Flemish city, which in the 15th century had become a European centre of commerce and a metropolis. The old medieval Town Hall, likewise in the marketplace, was no longer capable of accommodating the public functions of the city, and lacked the grandeur that was required.

This at any rate was how Antwerp city council saw it. In a let-ter to Philip II of Spain dated 29 August, 1560 applying for a new town hall, they complained that the old Town Hall was 'too confined, too small and too old'. Its condition had become 'so ruinous that to use it was to risk life and limb'. We may specu-late whether these arguments were put forward to justify demolishing and rebuilding a completely intact building. Con-temporary drawings show the Town Hall in excellent condition. Nonetheless, financing the new building posed no problems, all the necessary capital having been raised by the sale of annuity bonds carrying a relatively high guaranteed interest rate of between 7 and 10 per cent.

Cornelis Floris (1514–75), the brother of the famous painter Frans Floris (1519/20–70) was appointed architect, having emerged from the architectural competition as the winner. Unlike most of his contemporaries, details of the former's work as an artist and successful contractor are well known. Floris took responsibility for the design of the façade, but also oversaw construction. He is documented as having employed twelve sculptors and carvers on his own account. The ground plan, on the other hand, was drawn up by Hendrick van Paesschen and Jan Daems. Like many other buildings, therefore, Antwerp's Town Hall seems to have been a communal effort, even though Cornelis Floris, who was described in 1570 as 'a prince among architects', is the only one to have impressed his name on public awareness.

'Magnificent', 'dignified' and 'spacious' are words contem-poraries used to describe the finished building. Like Chambord (p. 68), it was ranked among the wonders of the world. Its archi-tecture, synthesising native traditions with models of Italian and French architecture – the Palazzo Grimani in Venice and the Château of Anet – into something quite new, became the flag-bearer of a new style. Its immediate successors were the Town Halls of Flushing and Emden.

Antwerp has thus been seen as the prototype of the modern-era town hall. It is no less than 255 ft wide, and though in its out-line it recalls the medieval town halls of Brussels, Louvain and Courtrai, its architectural details (a rusticated ground floor and columns and pilasters in the storeys above) are in the Renais-sance style. In combination with the inventive decorative pro-gramme of the façade – personifications of Wisdom and Justice at the sides and the Virgin in the middle as patron of the city – they immediately identified the building as a town hall. The balanced proportions and the precisely calculated use of deco-ration mark the high architectural status of Antwerp's Town Hall.

Unfortunately, nothing remains of the original interior, following phases of destruction and radical restoration under-taken in the 19th century.

Cornelis Floris
(Cornelius de Vriendt)

1513/14	Born in Antwerp
1538	Documented in Rome
c. 1548	Begins publishing influential series of engravings of ornaments
1550–52	Interior of the Church of St Leonardus in Zoutleeuw
1554	Active as a sculptor: tombs for Christian III of Denmark, in Roskilde, and Albert I of Brandenburg, in Königsberg (present-day Kaliningrad)
1573	Rood-screen in Tournai Cathedral
1575	Dies on 20 October

View of Antwerp Town Hall from the marketplace

Melchisedech van Hooren, *Stadhuis in Antwerpen*, 1565,
Albertina, Vienna

Ground plans before the alterations made in the 19th-century

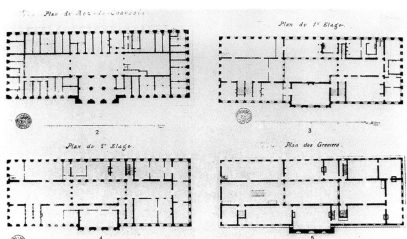

EL ESCORIAL
Juan Bautista de Toledo /
Juan de Herrera

Escorial, Spain, 1561–1581

The Escorial acted as a monastery, church, royal palace, burial vault, seminary, school, library, printing house, hospital and establishment where experiments were conducted in the natural sciences. It was the largest building project in 16th-century Spain. The location – about 25 miles from Madrid – was found only after two years of searching by a specially appointed team of scholars, including architects, geographers, geologists, philosophers and physicians. Together they helped to establish the criteria for the perfect site: the Hieronymite monks wanted a secluded monastery, but practical considerations meant it needed to be close to the Spanish capital. At the same time, copious reserves of water, plenty of accessible stone and forests supplying great quantities of building timber needed to be near at hand. The high altitude of the site (3,450 ft above sea level) ensured plenty of fresh air, but had the added advantage that it raised the monastery above the level of the religious centre of the country, the archbishopric of Toledo and the former capital. It was also said that the Escorial was the exact centre of Spain. Almost all the criteria matched the requirements for a well-chosen site according to Vitruvius's antique treatise on architecture, *De Architectura*.

Although the Escorial had to serve a wide range of functions, the ground plan is laid out on very clear principles. The central axis of the huge rectangle measuring 682 by 530 ft is broken up visually by the church and its forecourt. The church acted as both an oratory for the royal family and a monastic church. Its crypt is the burial vault of Spanish kings. To the south extended the buildings and courtyards of the monastery, to the north lay the palace, various schools and rooms for court servants. The most privileged location was occupied by the king and his family – the residential palace surrounded the choir of the monastic church. From his bed, the king could choose to look at either the main altar or an expansive landscape. Almost all the various functional areas of the Escorial were directly accessible via three doorways on the west side, only the ruler's palace being reached after passing through many forecourts and successions of rooms. This was at once the culmination and the end.

Comparisons have been made between the ground plan of the Escorial and hospital buildings of the 15th century, for example Antonio Filarete's Ospedale Maggiore built for Francesco Sforza in Milan (1456). Castle ground plans have also been cited. The grid structure has been interpreted as an allusion to the gridiron on which according to legend St Laurence was roasted. Philip II is supposed to have vowed to build the monastery on St Laurence's Day in 1557 (10 August), the day of his victory over the French at St Quentin. In every respect, the Escorial has many similarities with the description of the Temple of Solomon in the Bible, erected by the great Old Testament king himself. Thus, Philip would have seen himself as a builder in the tradition of the first and most notable ruler who was also an architect.

The design of the Escorial was in large measure conceived to suit the character of the grey granite with which it was built. The spare, calculated use of architectural detail merely enhances the impression it makes. A guiding principle was a desire for 'impressive simplicity', which was also appropriate to a monastic order. A description dating from 1605 stresses the monastery's 'plainness, exact concord of architectural features, noblesse without arrogance and majesty without ostentation'. Although the Escorial clearly borrows from Italian architecture – notable evidence being the doorway of the west front, which reflects the designs for Il Gesù in Rome (p. 124) – or could even be seen as a rival to St Peter's in Rome (p. 108), Philip II always

The vast granite complex of El Escorial: monastery, pantheon and palace in one

chose to stress the fundamentally Spanish character of the building. When Juan Bautista de Toledo's plans were sent to Florence for assessment after the first architect's death, Philip II wrote on their return: 'The expected plans from Italy have arrived, and they don't seem to contain anything of much use.'

View from the Guadarrama mountains

Abraham Ortelius, *Scenographia totius Fabricae S. Laurentii in Escorial*, etching, 1591

The library

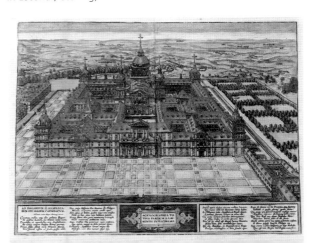

THE VILLA ROTONDA
Andrea Palladio

Vicenza, Italy, 1566–1570

Scarcely any Renaissance building has received as diverse a critical interpretation as La Rotonda, a country villa less than four miles from the gates of Vicenza, which Andrea Palladio built from 1566 for the retired ecclesiastic Paolo Almerico. It has variously been said to have been influenced by church architecture (because of the dome, i.e. the christianised Pantheon in Rome) or Norman palace architecture in Sicily. It has been described as a 'temple villa', obviously to explain the identical pillared porticoes on each side. Other terms used are 'belvedere' and 'villa suburbana'.

All these labels are linguistic attempts to pin down the architectural uniqueness of the villa. In a diary entry for 21 September, 1786, recording his journey through Italy, the German poet Johann Wolfgang von Goethe said of the Rotonda: 'Perhaps architecture has never taken luxury further.' This may have been because, unlike other Palladian villas and villa architecture of earlier periods, the building was not designed to be utilitarian – in other words it did not form the core of an agricultural estate and originally had no agricultural buildings attached. The guiding principle was to provide a raised architectural platform for viewing the landscape. According to classical descriptions of villas such as are found, for example, in the letters of Pliny the Younger around the turn of the first century AD, this may be considered a prime purpose of villa architecture in general.

Palladio himself wrote about the building in his architectural treatise, the *Quattro Libri dell'Architettura*, published in 1570: 'The site is among the most delightful and pleasant you could find. The house is set on an easily climbed hill bordered on one side by the navigable River Bacchiglione, on the other by more lovely hills that act as a huge theatre and are all such as produce plentiful fruit and excellent and good vines. As the views are wonderful on every side, some of them including surroundings close at hand, others extending further and others reaching right to the horizon, loggias have been built on all four sides.'

The mention of the surrounding hills as a 'theatre' likens the patron's position to being in a royal box, with the architecture as the director and the landscape as stage scenery. But there was a second, more practical reason for Palladio to position the building as he did – none of the four exterior walls is exposed to the sunlight or winds over its whole width.

The interior of the Rotonda has always been deemed unsatisfactory. Goethe called it 'liveable in but not cosy'. The layout with a central room has an unfavourable effect on the proportions of the subordinate corner rooms. The consensus view is reflected by the fact that, though there were numerous derivatives of the exterior in later architecture, for example Lord Burlington's Chiswick House of 1723–29, the interior arrangement was never copied.

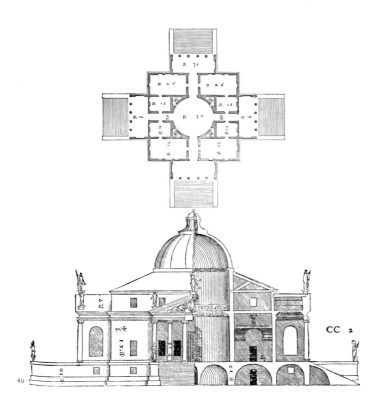

Andrea Palladio, ground plan and section, woodcut from *I Quattro Libri dell'Architettura*, 1570

The Villa Rotonda: a country house of perfect proportions just ouside the gates of Vicenza

Front view of the villa

COLOGNE TOWN HALL LOGGIA
Cornelis Floris and Wilhelm Vernukken

Cologne, Germany, 1567–1571

Following extensive bombing in World War II and further demolition in the 1960s, only three parts of Cologne's 'historic' Town Hall remain: one wall of the southern half of the Council Chamber on which 14th-century sculptures have been placed, the basement level and the southern half of the tower, constructed between 1407 and 1414. Also still extant is the Renaissance-style loggia, a masterpiece of the early modern era in northern Germany.

Yet the loggia survives only in its general features, because it was already 'dilapidated, in poor condition and ruinous' in the early 17th century and had to be 'rescued from collapse'. A vault was subsequently installed in the upper storey and armorial bearings were added to the projecting side pavilions. The heraldry was not reconstructed after it was destroyed in World War II. The 19th century brought the most extensive changes. In 1836, work began on replacing virtually all the masonry, and the steps to the upper storey were removed. Any assertion about the loggia must accordingly take into account the fact that the Town Hall is largely 19th century.

A loggia in front of the Town Hall was first documented in 1404. From 1477, written sources also tell us what it was used for. From the upper storey, new decrees and laws were proclaimed and thereby came into effect. By 1557, reconstruction was obviously envisaged: two drawings preserved in Cologne's municipal museum are dated to this year and bear the monogram 'C.F.' They are attributed to the architect of Antwerp's Town Hall (p. 116), Cornelis Floris. The second drawing in particular appears to record an early planning stage of the building erected ten years later under the direction of Wilhelm Vernukken. It would therefore appear that Vernukken merely added the projecting pavilions at the side but otherwise adhered largely to Floris's blueprint. He was thus less an architect than a stone mason and sculptor implementing another's ideas.

Unlike work carried out in other periods during the Renaissance, the Town Hall loggia was not overtly influenced by the Italian style, even if the architectural result was comparable. Though a two-storey loggia like the one in Cologne was under construction in the courtyard of the University of Padua (1546–87) and Palladio's Palazzo Chiericati (begun 1550) also introduced a feature of this sort, Renaissance influences during this period were largely transmitted across the Alps by means of Netherlandish intermediaries.

For Cologne, the Renaissance was wholly new. The loggia is appended to the main front of the Town Hall without any transition or accommodation of form or proportions. This merely enhances its otherness and novelty.

View of the Town Hall loggia. The previously flat-roofed upper storey received its Gothic rib vaulting in 1617/18

Johann Toussyn, *Councillors Entering the Town Hall Loggia,* (*left*) and *West View of the Town Hall* (*right*), both engravings from 1655

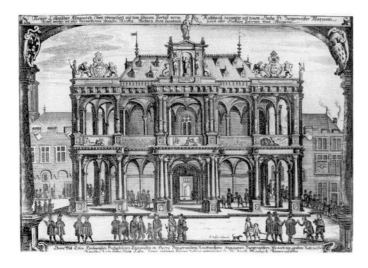

IL GESÙ
Giacomo Vignola / Giacomo della Porta

Rome, Italy, 1568–1584

Il Gesù is the first large church built by the Jesuits, who were approved as an order in 1540. Though the foundation stone was laid on 26 June, 1568, the history of the building goes back much further. Originally there was a small church on the south-eastern edge of the ancient Campus Martius, about a quarter of a mile from the Capitol. In 1549, it was decided to build a much larger church, but because of land ownership disputes this was never realized. Six years later, work was begun on a church to plans by Michelangelo, by then almost an octagenarian. This work was also suspended. In the meantime, the founder of the order, Ignatius Loyola, died, and no-one stood behind the project any longer.

It was not until the new Cardinal Protector of the Order, Alessandro Farnese (1520–89), supported the project that funding finally became available. Writing to Vignola (cf. p. 110), who had been appointed architect, the new promoter wrote on 26 August, 1568: 'To Vignola. The design of the church must be such that it is well proportioned in length, breadth and height in accordance with the rules of good architecture, but without exceeding the budget. The church must not be a basilica with aisles, but a nave with chapels on each side. I want the church to be aligned in any event so that the façade with its front is oriented to the street. And the church must be vaulted and nothing else. Keep well.' As if from a catalogue, the architect had previously offered the client various designs to choose from: a building with an oval ground plan or a solution with a rectangular, elongated ground plan. Farnese had plumped for the latter variant. With its simple yet clear spatial structure, it would become the prototype of Catholic Church architecture elsewhere in Europe (p. 130).

The interior of the church is harmonious and well proportioned: the nave is twice as long as it is wide; the crossing and choir together are the same length as the nave. The present-day spatial impression is largely the result of 17th-century additions, with impressive ceiling frescoes by Giovanni Battista Gaulli and altars by Andrea Pozzo and Pietro da Cortona. And yet it is the original plan by Vignola that makes the church what it is, with the sacrament at the altar the functional focus of the design.

Vignola's design of the façade was not carried out, criticised mainly for lacking reference to the interior of the church. Even so, it was published as an engraving in 1573. The façade that was realised was designed by Michelangelo's pupil Giacomo della Porta. Comparing Vignola's design with the actual façade, the innovative tendency of della Porta's thinking is evident. Heralding the forthcoming transition to a Baroque style, his façade is charged with far greater energy – he used linked columns and pilasters and generally greater decorative detail to dramatise the central section. The principle of a dynamic intensification was thus given equal importance alongside the previously all-important ideal of the balance of proportions.

Giacomo della Porta

1532	Born in Porlezza
1559	First mentioned as a sculptor
1564	Appointed 'Architect of the Roman People'
1574	Constructs various fountains in Rome
1588–1603	Dome of St Peter's, following Michelangelo's plans
1602	Dies on 3 September in Rome

Valérien Regnard, engraving showing the façade with ground plan and a view of the interior, 1622

The façade of the Jesuit church Il Gesù, completed to the design of Giacomo della Porta in 1577

The interior of the church with its 17th-century decoration

THE HALL OF ANTIQUITIES
Jacopo Strada

The Residence, Munich, Germany, begun 1569

The Hall of Antiquities (Antiquarium) was incorporated into the Munich Residence as late as the 17th century. Previously it was detached from the palace and externally rather unprepossessing. It was first constructed by the Bavarian Duke Albert v (1528–79) as a home for his collection of antique sculpture. A rather ambivalent description of the inside survives from 1611: 'I've never seen so many antiquities together in one room, not even in Rome or Florence.' By then the building had already lost its original purpose as one of the earliest museums anywhere and, a mere twenty years after work started, it served as a general-purpose, grand function room.

And yet people continued to come just to see the famous antique sculptures, most of them assembled by the Italian scholar Jacopo Strada. The German poet Johann Wolfgang von Goethe recorded his impressions of a visit on 6 September, 1786. He wrote: 'In the antiquities room, I really noticed that my eyes lack practice at looking at objects like this, so I had no wish to linger and waste time. Much of it said nothing to me, without my being able to determine why. A Drusus caught my attention, and two attractive Antoninuses and a few other things appealed to me. Overall, the things are not even well laid out.'

Along with the Hall of Antiquities, the upper storey of which was intended to accommodate the substantial ducal library, Albert v ordered work to begin on an art cabinet for his pictures and collection of valuables, a building now known as the Münze (Mint). These two buildings were the first autonomous buildings in European art history intended specifically to house art collections. Jacopo Strada, whom Titian painted in a famous portrait now in the Kunsthistorisches Museum in Vienna, is considered the creator of the Hall of Antiquities. In the introduction to a book dedicated to the duke in 1575, Strada reminded Albert: 'But when it was resolved to bring the library and the

antiques together in a suitable, fire-proof place, an ample, detached, purpose-built palace building was constructed at your behest, the whole interior of which was designed by me. There are two spacious rooms in it. The lower one displays a plaster ceiling, with antiques standing here and there in not inappropriate order. The upper one is decorated with fine, lavishly carved panelling – this is the library, which can never be adequately praised.'

This indicates that the art collector and humanist Strada designed the collection and the way it was presented. Responsible for the design and construction of the Hall of Antiquities were Simon Zwitzel of Augsburg and the duke's court architect Wilhelm Egckl.

The somewhat oppressive character of the Hall of Antiquities, in which the huge barrel vaulting reaches right down to the level of the projecting wall piers, can be seen as a visual translation of Strada's emphatic requirement for fire proofing. In fact the room, which is nearly 230 ft long and over 33 ft wide, is in a real sense without precedent, even though buildings such as the Belvedere in Prague (p. 92), the gallery in the château at Fontainebleau (p. 76) or the library at San Lorenzo in Florence (p. 70) may well have served as models to a certain extent. This also underlines the international horizon that Munich architecture had reached by the late 16th century.

Jacopo Strada

c. 1515	Born in Mantua
1547	Documented as active goldsmith
c. 1544–56	Commissions from the Fuggers in Augsburg
1557	First journey to Italy to purchase classical works of art
1553	Writes comprehensive book on numismatics
1559/60	Consulted in connection with the work on the tomb of the Emperor Maximilian I in Innsbruck
1588	Dies in Vienna, probably in November

Johann Matthias Kager, south wall of doorway, pen and ink drawing, 1611

View of the Hall of Antiquities

The palace façade fronting the Residenzstrasse,
completed in 1616

Detail of wall frieze with classical busts

IL REDENTORE
Andrea Palladio

Venice, Italy, 1577–1592

Andrea Palladio's labours for the Serenissima have been described as a 'chronicle of failure'. He was not appointed to the official post of state architect that he sought, his designs for private palaces were not built and his pioneering ideas for the rebuilding of the Rialto bridge likewise remained on the drawing board. Nor was he invited to take part in the grand scheme of 1557 to make Venice 'the finest city in the world'. His achievements in Venice were limited to erecting buildings on the perimeter of the city. The churches he designed were for clients based outside Venice.

And yet, once a year, Palladio's church of Il Redentore is the most important building in the city. Every third Sunday in July since 1578, a bridge of boats has been set up to carry a procession over the Giudecca canal into the church. The occasion for the procession is the same as for building the church: in the autumn of 1576 the Republic vowed to construct a votive church in thanksgiving for deliverance from a devastating plague which had claimed the lives of over 50,000 Venetians – hence the name of the church, which derives from the Latin word 'redemptor', signifying 'saviour'. In design and dimensions, its architecture is geared to accommodate a mass congregation. A broad flight of steps leads into a huge, triumphal arch-style entrance portico recessed into the façade. The design derives from the Pantheon in Rome, which was also the inspiration for the dome. The latter's flanking bell-towers, on the other hand, hark back to Romanesque architecture or even minarets.

The interior of Il Redentore is a peristyle hall. A rhythmic sequence of wall piers articulate the nave, while the sanctuary is distinguished by four full columns. Behind this is the choir for the Capucin monks who were to care of the church. The various functional areas form a subtly evolving architectural drama from the entrance to the interior, each with its own spatial characteristics. The arrangement is quite different from Giacomo Vignola's Il Gesù, his most important church building (p. 124) of roughly the same period, which is incidentally far more momentous historically in that the whole interior focuses on a single point, i.e. the high altar, where the sacrifice of the mass takes place. Il Redentore had, in contrast, to serve several functions – the building had to accommodate a lay congregation, monks and the processional service. Here, Palladio improved on artistic ideas he had developed for his other important church commission in Venice, San Giorgio Maggiore (begun 1566). Il Redentore is thus justly designated as his architectural masterpiece.

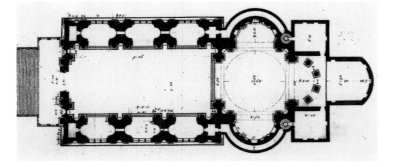

Ground plan

Andrea Palladio
(Andrea di Pietro della Gondola)

1508   Born on 19 August in Padua
1521   Apprenticeship as stonemason and sculptor
1541   First of a total of four trips to Rome
1542   Villa Godi-Malinverni in Lonedo di Lugo. First example of his own work
1570   First edition of his treatise on architecture called *I quattro libri dell' architettura*
1579   San Giorgio Maggiore in Venice
1580   Theatro Olympico in Vicenza
1580   Andrea Palladio dies on 19 August in Vicenza

View of the votive church from across the Grand Canal

Il Redentore viewed from the side

The interior with its slender columns

JESUIT CHURCH OF ST MICHAEL
Friedrich Sustris and Wendel Dietrich

Munich, Germany, 1583–1597

In 1582, one of Germany's leading rulers of the day, Duke William V of Bavaria (1548–1626), decided to erect a Jesuit college in the middle of Munich dedicated to the Archangel Michael. The duke had succeeded in converting the archbishop of Cologne to Catholicism, and now it was a matter of ensuring that Munich, which likewise threatened to become Protestant, returned to the fold.

The college that was built in the following years was the largest homogeneous structure in the city. In its architecture, it is oriented to the repertoire of Italian palazzo façades. A contemporary described it as being 'so large that a king could hold court in it. It has courts and gardens of various sizes, large and small rooms in great number, pretty bedrooms, dining rooms, schools and rooms with blackboards in which the young people hear mass every day. The college has 800 windows and is, so the Rector tells me, the noblest in Europe after the Escorial in Spain. The fathers owe everything to his Grace Duke William.'

The college church is described as the progenitor of modern church architecture in Germany, an inspiration for every Jesuit church in southern Germany, Westphalia, the Rheinland and even Alsace in the 17th and early 18th centuries. This is due not least to the circumstance that the building drawings for Jesuit churches had to be sent to the headquarters in Rome, where the primary emphasis was on recognisable, standard images. Planning began in 1582. According to a ground plan now at the Bibliothèque Nationale in Paris, the original intention was a three-aisled hall church in the Gothic style. But virtually overnight plans changed. The assumption is that the Jesuits in Rome intervened. At any rate, by 1597 the church that resulted followed the model of Il Gesù in Rome (p. 124) and San Fedele in Milan. In 1611, the church was therefore described quite logically as being 'built in the Italian manner'.

Critics have always scratched their heads over the façade, calling it mean, severe and even awkward. Objectively considered, it resembles a contemporary Central European town hall more than a church. And the rich programme of inscriptions and statues that could only have been intelligible to a thoroughly educated man of the day give it a character all of its own. Saintly images mingle with those of rulers past and present. As if in an ancestral gallery, there are sculptures of Constantine, Charlemagne, Charles V and Duke William himself, all featuring as champions of the Catholic faith. And the bronze figure of St

Michael by Hubert Gerhard (1588), thrusting his apostate colleague Lucifer out of heaven, must also be seen as a symbol of the Counter-Reformation. The iconographical programme turned the façade into an instrument of propaganda.

On the other hand, the interior with its huge barrel vaulting, spanning some 65 ft, has always been seen as a high point of architectural history. The Italian models of Il Gesù and Sant'Andrea in Mantua (p. 28), and even classical buildings such as the Baths of Diocletian, took on their own individual form in this building. The interplay of light and shadow is incomparable and the white stuccowork, though somewhat clumsily restored after the damage the church sustained in World War II, is of outstanding quality.

The building history of the church is as complex as the interior. The architects Friedrich Sustris and Wendel Dietrich played a part in getting work underway, a certain Wolf Miller oversaw construction and a number of internationally renowned figures also spent time on site dispensing professional advice. Finally, the figurative programme on the façade was conceived by the duke himself, who wrote the inscriptions as well.

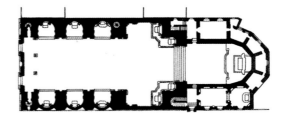

Ground plan

Friedrich Sustris

c. 1540	Born, probably in Venice
1563–67	Active in Florence as a painter
1573–	Commissions from the Wittelsbach court in Bavaria
1599	Dies in Munich

Wendel Dietrich

c. 1535	Born in Augsburg
1557	First documented in Augsburg tax registers
1569–	Commissions from the Fugger family, mainly for furniture
1586–89	High altar and choir stalls, the Church of St Michael, Munich
1622	Dies in Augsburg

View down the nave
towards the choir

Detail of the façade with the statue of St Michael by
Hubert Gerhard between the two portals

View from Neuhauserstrasse

JULEUM
Paul Francke

Helmstedt, Germany, 1592–1597

The University of Helmstedt was founded by Duke Julius of Brunswick-Lüneberg (1528–89) in 1575. Though the fact is not generally appreciated today, it developed into one of the most important universities in the German-speaking world and, for a time, was the third largest. Giordano Bruno taught here in 1589/90 and in 1799 the mathematician Carl Friedrich Gauss graduated from Helmstedt. In 1810, the university was closed, having been superseded by Göttingen as the duchy's major university.

As with other universities, such as Marburg and Göttingen, former monastic properties were made available to house the university. In Helmstedt, work began in 1577/78 on a site previously belonging to the Mariental monastery, using parts of existing monastic ranges to develop two wings. These enclose the western and eastern sides of an elongated rectangular courtyard. The bottom floors are of solid stone, supporting half-timbered upper storeys above that were rebuilt in the 17th century. In front of the two wings are octagonal stair towers, the western one, which contains the rooms of the liberal arts faculty, being endowed with a splendid doorway. Here, as at every other university, a combination of philosophy, language studies and natural sciences formed the basis of career-oriented studies.

The final development (1592–97) was the construction of the principal building, named the Juleum in honour of the founder, on the north side by court architect Paul Francke. It served as a lecture hall for the three 'higher' faculties (theology, medicine and jurisprudence), and also contained the library. As was mentioned at the ceremonial opening of the Juleum on 15 October, 1612, that the functional arrangement of the buildings followed that of Oxford's 14th-century New College. In aesthetic terms, i.e. in the axisymmetrical disposition of its detached buildings, the inspiration was found in architectural books of the 16th century, such as in Hans Vredemann de Vries's *Architectura* of 1563. The Capitol in Rome (p. 90) may also have been influential.

The architectural detail, such as the splendidly ornate gables and heavily decorated window and door surrounds, identify the Juleum as an ambitious showpiece and principal building of the university. Unlike in Netherlandish and Italian Renaissance architecture, columns are used only as decorative features. The building itself is not over fussy and is a straightforward combination of two principal storeys and five vertical axes. The most striking feature is the 183-ft tower in the centre and the sculptural decoration, most of which was provided by the multitalented sculptor Adam Liquier.

A century ago, the Juleum was acclaimed to be 'one of the best buildings of the period'. It was in any event the first German university building of the modern era.

Plan of the first floor, prior to rebuilding as a library, Niedersächsisches Staatsarchiv, Wolfenbüttel

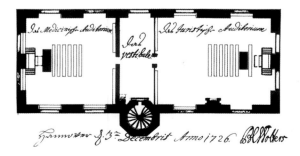

Paul Francke

1538	Born in Weimar, Gemany
1573–	Architect in the service of the dukes of Brunswick-Wolfenbüttel
1608	Work begins on the Church of Our Lady in Wolfenbüttel. First Protestant civic church in Germany
1615	Dies in Wolfenbüttel

View of the Juleum and its wings

The main building, the so-called Juleum

Extravagantly decorated portal in the west wing

Door surrounds on the main building

THE GREAT ARMOURY

Gdańsk, Poland, 1593–1612

The Great Armoury in Gdańsk is one of the most outstanding works of architecture of the period around 1600. In size and splendour there is scarcely any building in the region to compare it with. Contemporaries showered it with superlatives – in 1645, it was an 'ornament of the city', two years later it was 'one of finest things to look at in existence'. Unfortunately, the building no longer receives the appreciation it deserves. This may have to do with its original function as an arsenal, but more pertinent is the history of its preservation. In 1945, only the foundations remained standing (cf. p. 12), and subsequent rebuilding was carried out with limited success. Polution has also had a negative effect on what little that survives of the original fabric.

As an arsenal, the Armoury of course served to store weapons. It was a type of building that developed only in the second half of the 15th century. Previously, weapons had been stored in forts, town halls or even churches. Examples of this widespread type of building are found in almost every large town. In Graz, Austria, for example, even the original interior furnishings of an armoury have been reconstructed.

In buildings of this kind, the low ground floor was generally used to store and maintain artillery. There could be up to five further floors for lighter weapons, armour and other defensive equipment, with the weight of the stored objects declining with each higher floor. Accordingly, armouries would seem to have been primarily functional buildings designed to make weapons quickly available. This also applies to the Great Armoury in Gdańsk, planned in 1593 and built between 1600 and 1612. Erected directly beside the western fortifications of the city, it has a huge, four-aisled ground floor that can be reached via four doorways. Two stair towers at the ends of the main front lead up to the upper floors. Exclusively practical considerations seem to have been to the fore in planning the building.

Yet a fountain in front of the west façade, a niche with a statue of the Roman goddess Minerva and the rich sculptural decoration of the doorways and gables show that the Armoury was intended as far more than a purely utilitarian building. The reason for the display was probably the city's desire to emphasise its military autonomy vis-à-vis the Polish monarchy as a result of its special political status. Only a few decades before work started on the Armoury, the city's independence had been the subject of bitter disputes between the city and the crown. Obviously it was hoped that anyone seeing the building would note its prominence as a visible statement of the city's self-reliance.

In its external features, the structure is in the tradition of the richly decorated urban façades of the Netherlands, such as Haarlem's meat hall. Specific motifs were drawn from the palaces at Rosenborg and Frederiksborg in Denmark. Netherlandish architecture had become well known over a wide area in the second half of the 17th century through engravings, especially those by Hans Vredeman de Vries. In the run-up to the planning process for the Armoury, Vredeman de Vries was actually summoned to Gdansk, but failed to secure the commission for himself. For a long time, it was thought that Mechelen-born Antonius von Obbergen was the architect, following his completion of the palace of Kronborg near Helsingör in Denmark and his work on the palace in Kostrzyn. However, Obbergen is not mentioned in a single document connected with the building. It is therefore likely that the authors of the Armoury were masons and sculptors, especially Wilhelm Barth the Younger, Abraham van den Blocke and Philip Schumacher.

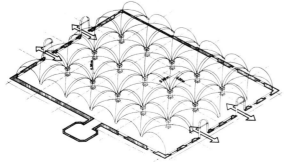

Isometric projection of the ground floor

The Great Armoury, Danzig: the east façade

The west façade

The east façade, etching by Matthäus Deisch, from a drawing by Friedrich August Anton Lohrmann, 1761–65

AUGSBURG TOWN HALL
Elias Holl

Augsburg, Germany, 1614–1620

Augsburg's Town Hall is among the masterpieces of 17th-century secular architecture in Germany. A virtually complete record of the building's history exists owing to a relatively high number of documentary sources, several drawings and four architectural models from the construction period. Some questions, however, remain open – for example, why were plans made to rebuild the medieval town hall in 1609–10, when a mere four years later was decided on a grandiose new building? The cost of the latter was so high that it swallowed up no less than four per cent of the city's total budget for several years.

At the time, the city was at the time not in a particularly good way economically: high inflation loomed and the city's political importance continued to wane. In the 16th century, the Imperial Diet (Reichstag) frequently convened in Augsburg. Now Regensburg supplanted it as one of the most important cities in the Holy Roman Empire, at least politically. Under these circumstances, the construction of the new Augsburg Town Hall might therefore have been seen as an investment in the future, staking out the city's claim to national importance.

The Town Hall was described in the 17th century as 'magnificent', 'stately' and 'distinguished'. In 1644, it was said that its capaciousness was comparable to paradise, and the councillors' rooms were 'majestic and worthy of a king'. The architect, Augsburg's municipal architect Elias Holl, said that he wanted to construct a 'bold' and 'heroic' building. Clearly these words helped him to convince the city council in 1618 to add two more towers. The cost of these alone would have been enough to erect a separate medium-sized building.

Beside the towers, which heightened the effect of the structure by lending it monumentality, the raised centre section with its diminutive pediment towers dominates the elegant and sparingly decorated façade. It emphasises the six central bays, behind which is the Golden Room, the central assembly room occupying three storeys, which was completely destroyed in World War II. This is where the city council was elected and met, and also where celebrations and receptions were held.

The Town Hall's decorative programme culminates in the Golden Room. The gilt walnut ceiling depicts the Triumph of Wisdom, which is accompanied by personifications of Justice, Courage, Peace, Mercy and Wealth. When they convened, the city councillors had these emblematic figures before them as an exhortation to good government serving the general well-being of the people.

The monumental architecture of the Town Hall as such is without antecedent, although individual motifs can be traced back to various sources. The combination of rectangular and oval windows, for example, was borrowed from the Jesuit college built a few decades earlier in Munich (p. 130), while many ground plan features derive ultimately from Vitruvius's architectural treatise *De Architectura*. However, the box-like character of the design, in which individual motifs are subordinated to the overall effect, is an innovation unique to the Augsburg Town Hall. Aspects of Baroque architecture appear to be anticipated here.

In 1905, it was said on this point: 'The whole importance of the building lies in the prodigal silhouette and the force and mass of the cube. These roundly declare that, plain though it may be, this building is where power lies.'

Elias Holl

1573	Born on 28 February, the son of a family of architects and masons in Augsburg, Germany
1596	Qualifies as master on 25 May. Previously works with his father on architectural projects
1600/1601	Travels to Italy
1601–	Various building projects in and around Augsburg
1602	Augsburg city architect
c. 1635	Writes on architecture
1646	Dies in Augsburg on 6 January

Theodor Fischer, perspective cross-section of Augsburg Town Hall, 1886

The seat of power: Elias Holl's Town Hall in Augsburg

The Golden Hall: completely
destroyed during World
War II, it was reconstructed
as an exact replica in 1985

THE BANQUETING HOUSE
Inigo Jones

Whitehall, London, England, 1619–1622

In 1605, while travelling in Italy, Inigo Jones (1573–1652) was given Bordino's work *De Rebus pracclare* by an English resident, the historian Edmund Bolton whose personal dedication seems to have been a wish and a challenge in equal measure: 'sculpture, modelling, architecture, painting, acting and all that is praiseworthy in the elegant arts of the ancients may one day find their way across the Alps into our England.'

The Banqueting House in Whitehall, the first and only part of Jones's proposed rebuilding of the medieval palace of Whitehall actually constructed, fulfilled this wish. As the finest and justly most famous work by Jones, it draws on many ideas of classical architecture. The direct inspiration is the work of Andrea Palladio and the architecture of the Palazzo Thiene and Palazzo Valmarana in Vicenza which Jones had visited. Jones's personal copy of Palladio's *Quattro Libri dell'Architettura* with detailed annotations still survives.

The Banqueting House was originally used for masques and other spectacles. The first such building had been constructed to the designs of Thomas Graves in 1581. In 1609, it was rebuilt to plans by Robert Smythson, though Inigo Jones may already have been involved in this. It consisted of a large hall containing a gallery supported on Ionic columns. In 1619 this building burnt down. Jones took only three months to draw up plans for a replacement structure consisting of a large hall with galleries, to dimensions that obviously largely replicated the earlier building. In 1636, the ceilings were painted by Peter Paul Rubens (1577–1640) with a highly political series of paintings extolling the Stuart monarchy. Since the paintings were both expensive and fragile, masques and the like were then banned and the hall used for ceremonial state occasions, as it still is.

The façade of the Banqueting House is two-storeyed, divided into seven bays. The three centre bays are decorated with columns, the side bays with pilasters. Originally, different sorts of stone ranging from honey yellow through brown to white provided a polychrome exterior, but radical restorations in the 18th and 19th centuries left the building with its present white Portland stone exterior. The balanced, harmonious proportions of the building were admired from the first. In 1715, it was said that 'our excellent Inigo Jones here combined severity with elegance, adornment with simplicity and beauty with grandeur. The Banqueting House is undoubtedly the best building in the world.'

Inigo Jones

1573	Baptised on 19 July in London
1598–1604	Tours Europe
1605–6	Returns to Italy
1605–40	Designs stage sets for court masques
1616–19	Designs Queen's House, Greenwich
1623–25	Queen's Chapel, St James's Palace, London
1631	St Paul's, Covent Garden, London
1652	Dies on 21 June in London

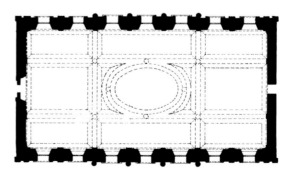

Ground plan

The façade of the Banqueting House facing Whitehall

Architect's drawing from 1619

The Throne Room and Banqueting Hall

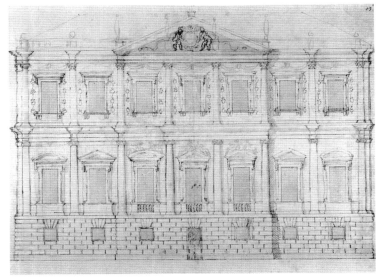

BIBLIOGRAPHY

Primary Literature

Leon Battista Alberti, *De re aedificatoria* (1485). Ed. Giovanni Orlandi. Milan, 1966 (English edition 1988).

Jacques Androuet du Cerceau. *Les plus excellents Bastiments de France* (1576/77). Repr. 1972 (English edition 1988).

Philibert de l'Orme. *Le premier Tome d'architecture* (1567). Ed. Gert Bekaert. Brussels, 1981.

Andrea Palladio. *I Quattro Libri dell'Architettura* (1570). Ed. Licisco Magagnato and Paola Marini. Milan, 1980 (English edition 1997).

Sebastiano Serlio. *Regole generali di architettura sopra le cinque maniere degli edifici*. Venice, 1537.

Giorgio Vasari. *Le Vite de' più eccellenti architetti, pittori, et scultori italiani* (1550 and 1568). Ed. Rosanna Bettarini. Florence, 1966ff. (English edition 1976).

Jacopo Barozzi da Vignola. *Regola delli cinque ordini d'architettura* (1562). Repr. Vignola, 1974.

Secondary Literature and Encyclopaedia

James S. Ackerman. *The Villa: Form and Ideology of Country Houses*. London, 1990.

Allgemeines Künstlerlexikon: Die Bildenden Künstler aller Zeiten und Völker. Munich and Leipzig, 1983ff.

Daniel Arasse and Andreas Tönnesmann. *Der europäische Manierismus 1520–1610*. Munich, 1997.

Jan Bialostocki. *The Art of the Renaissance in Eastern Europe: Hungary, Bohemia, Poland*. Oxford, 1976.

Hartmut Biermann. *Renaissance*. Munich, 1976.

Arnoldo Bruschi (ed.). *Storia dell'architettura Italiana: Il Primo Cinquecento*. Milan, 2002.

August Buck (ed.). *Zu Begriff und Problem der Renaissance*. Darmstadt, 1969.

Jacob Burckhardt. *Die Kultur der Renaissance in Italien: Ein Versuch*. Basle, 1860.

The Dictionary of Art. Ed. Jane Turner. London, 1996.

Francesco Paolo Fiore (ed.). *Storia dell'architettura Italiana: Il Quattrocento*. Milan, 1996.

Hubertus Günther. *Das Studium der antiken Architektur in den Zeichnungen der Hochrenaissance*. Tübingen, 1988.

Ludwig Heinrich Heydenreich and Wolfgang Lotz. *Architecture in Italy 1400–1600*. New Haven, CT, and London 1974.

Henry-Russell Hitchcock. *German Renaissance Architecture*. Princeton, NJ, 1983.

Thomas DaCosta Kaufmann. *Court, Cloister & City: The Art and Culture of Central Europe 1450–1800*. London, 1995.

Spiro Kostof (ed.). *The Architect: Chapters in the History of the Profession*. New York and Oxford, 1977.

Hanno-Walter Kruft. *A History of Architectural Theory: From Vitruvius to the Present*. London, 1994.

Fernando Marías. *El Siglo XVI: Gótico y Rinascimento*. Madrid, 1992.

Henry Millon et al. (eds). *The Renaissance from Brunelleschi to Michelangelo: The Representation of Architecture*. London, 1994.

Matthias Müller. 'Die Tradition als subversive Kraft: Beobachtungen zur Rezeption italienischer Renaissanceelemente im französischen und deutschen Schlossbau'. In Norbert Nussbaum, Stefan Hoppe et al. (eds). *Wege zur Renaissance: Beobachtungen zu den Anfängen neuzeitlicher Kunstauffassung im Rheinland und in den Nachbargebieten*. Cologne, 2002.

Frédérique Pauwels-Lemerle and Yves Pauwels-Lemerle. *L'Architecture à la Renaissance*. Paris, 1998.

Wolfram Prinz and Ronald G. Kecks. *Das französische Schloss der Renaissance*. Berlin, 1985.

Bernd Roeck. *Kunstpatronage in der Frühen Neuzeit. Studien zu Kunstmarkt, Künstlern und ihren Auftraggebern in Italien und im Heiligen Römischen Reich (15.–17. Jahrhundert)*. Göttingen, 1999.

Anna Schunicht-Rave and Vera Lüpkes (eds). *Handbuch der Renaissance: Deutschland, Niederlande, Belgien, Österreich*. Cologne, 2002.

Christof Thoenes. 'Opus incertum': *Italienische Studien aus drei Jahrzehnten*. Munich, 2002.

Andreas Tönnesmann. 'Art: Renaissance'. In *Der Neue Pauly: Enzyklopädie der Antike*. Ed. V. Manfred Landfester. Vol. 15/2. Stuttgart and Weimar, 2002.

Ulrich Thieme and Felix Becker (eds). *Allgemeines Lexikon der bildenden Künstler von der Antike bis zur Gegenwart*. Leipzig, 1907–50.

Gerrit Walther. 'Adel und Antike: Zur politischen Bedeutung gelehrter Kultur für die Führungselite der Frühen Neuzeit'. *Historische Zeitschrift* 266 (1998), pp. 359–85.

Rudolf Wittkower. *Architectural Principles in the Age of Humanism*. London, 1949.

Henri Zerner. *L'Art de la Renaissance en France l'invention du classicisme*. Paris, 1996.

Secondary Literature (listed according to architect)

LEON BATTISTA ALBERTI

Eugene S. Johnson. *Sant'Andrea in Mantua: The Building History*. University Park, 1975.

Hellmut Lorenz. 'Zur Architektur L.B. Albertis: Die Kirchenfassaden'. *Wiener Jahrbuch für Kunstgeschichte* 29 (1976), pp. 65–100.

Giovanni Rucellai ed il suo Zibaldone. Vol. 2: *A Florentine Patrician and his Palace: Studies*. London, 1981.

Robert Tavernor. *On Alberti and the Art of Building*. New Haven, CT, and London, 1998.

Stefano Ugo Baldassarri and Arielle Saiber (eds). *Images of Quattrocento Florence: Selected Writings in Literature, History, and Art*. New Haven, CT and London, 2000, pp. 246–51.

DONATO BRAMANTE

Arnoldo Bruschi. *Bramante*. London, 1973.

Hubertus Günther. *Bramantes Tempietto: Die Memorialanlage der Kreuzigung Petri in S. Pietro in Montorio, Rom*. Munich, 1973.

Ulrich Kahle. *Renaissance-Zentralbauten in Oberitalien: Santa Maria Presso San Satiro: Das Frühwerk Bramantes in Mailand*. Munich, 1982.

Nicole Riegel. 'San Pietro in Montorio in Rom: Die Votivkirche der spanischen Könige Isabella und Ferdinand von Spanien'. *Römisches Jahrbuch der Bibliotheca Herziana* 32 (1997/98), pp. 273–320.

FILIPPO BRUNELLESCHI

Heinrich Klotz. *Frühwerke Brunelleschis und die mittelalterliche Tradition*. Berlin, 1970.

Helmut Lorenz et al. 'Santo Spirito und das Spätwerk Brunelleschis'. In Lars Olaf Larsson and Götz Pochat (eds). *Kunstgeschichtliche Studien zur Florentiner Renaissance*. Stockholm, 1980, pp. 87–143.

Howard Saalman. *Filippo Brunelleschi: The Buildings*. London, 1993.

Cristina Acidini Luchinat (ed.). *La Chiesa e il Convento di Santo Spirito a Firenze*. Florence, 1996.

GIULIO ROMANO

Kurt W. Forster and Richard Tuttle. 'The Palazzo del Te'. *Journal of the Society of Architectural Historians* 30 (1971), pp. 267–93.

Egon Verheyen. *The Palazzo del Te in Mantua: Images of Love and Politics*. Baltimore, 1977.

Sergio Polano (ed.). *Giulio Romano*. Milan, 1989.

ELIAS HOLL

Elias Holl und das Augsburger Rathaus. Ed. Wolfram Baer. Exh. cat. Regensburg, 1985.

Bernd Roeck. *Elias Holl: Architekt einer europäischen Stadt.* Regensburg, 1985.

——. 'AMPLISS: REPVB. AVGVSTANAE ARCHIETCTVS': Augsburg und sein Stadtwerkmeister: Einige Anmerkungen zum Forschungsstand'. In Markus Hörsch and Elisabeth Oy-Marra (eds). *Kunst, Macht, Politik: Festschrift für Franz Matsche zum 60. Geburtstag,* Petersberg, 2000, pp. 69–76.

INIGO JONES

John Summerson. *Inigo Jones.* Harmondsworth, 1966.

The King's Arcadia: Inigo Jones and the Stuart Court. Ed. John Harris et al. Exh. cat. London, 1973.

Roy Strong. *Britannia Triumphans: Inigo Jones, Rubens and the Whitehall Palace.* London, 1980.

John Harris and Gordon Higgot. *Inigo Jones: Complete Architectural Drawings.* London, 1989.

HIERONYMUS LOTTER

Lutz Unbehaun. *Der sächsische Baumeister Hieronymus Lotter.* Leipzig, 1989.

Wolfram Günther. *Hieronymus Lotter.* In Arnold Bartetzky (ed.) *Die Baumeister der 'Deutschen Renaissance.' Ein Mythos der Baugeschichte?* Beucha bei Leipzig, 2003.

MICHELANGELO BUONAROTTI

James S. Ackerman. *The Architecture of Michelangelo.* London, 1961.

Herbert von Einem. *Michelangelo: Bildhauer, Maler, Baumeister.* Berlin, 1973.

Harmen Thies. *Michelangelo: Das Kapitol.* Florence, 1982.

William E. Wallace. *Michelangelo at San Lorenzo: The Genius as Entrepreneur.* Cambridge, 1994.

PHILIBERT DE L'ORME

Anthony Blunt. *Philibert de l'Orme.* London, 1958.

Jean-Marie Pérouse de Montclos. *Philibert de L'Orme: Architecte du roi (1514–1570).* Paris, 2000.

ANDREAS PALLADIO

Wolfgang Lotz. 'La Rotonda, edificio civile con cupola'. *Bollettino del Centro Internazionale di Studi di Architettura Andrea Palladio* 4 (1962), pp. 69–73.

James S. Ackerman. *Palladio: The Architect and Society.* Harmondsworth, 1966.

——. *Palladio's Villas.* Locust Valley, 1967.

Wladimir Timofiewitsch. *Die sakrale Architektur Palladios.* Munich, 1968.

Bruce Boucher. *Andrea Palladio: The Architect in his Time.* New York, 1994.

SEBASTIANO SERLIO

Christof Thoenes (ed.). *Sebastiano Serlio.* Milan, 1989.

Sabine Frommel. *Sebastiano Serlio Architetto.* Milan, 1998.

GIORGIO VASARI

Johanna Lessmann. *Studien zu einer Baumonographie der Uffizien Giorgio Vasaris in Florenz.* Bonn, 1975.

Leon George Satkowski. *Giorgio Vasari: Architect and Courtier.* Princeton, NJ, 1993.

Patricia Lee Rubin. *Giorgio Vasari: Art and History.* New Haven, CT, and London, 1995.

GIACOMO BAROZZI DA VIGNOLA

Christof Thoenes. 'Versuch über Architektur und Gesellschaft im Werk Vignolas'. *Kritische Berichte* (1987), pp. 5–19.

Richard J. Tuttle et al. (eds). *Jacopo Barozzi da Vignola.* Milan, 2002.

Secondary Literature (listed according to place)

ANET

Sigrid Ruby. 'Diane de Poitiers (1500–1566)'. In Margarete Zimmermann and Roswitha Böhm (eds). *Französische Frauen der Frühen Neuzeit: Dichterinnen, Malerinnen, Mäzeninnen.* Darmstadt, 1999, pp. 45–54.

ANTWERP

Holm Bevers. *Das Rathaus von Antwerpen (1561–1565): Architektur und Figurenprogramm.* Hildesheim et al., 1985.

Wouter Kuyper. *The Triumphant Entry of Renaissance Architecture into the Netherlands: The Joyeuse Entrée of Philip of Spain into Antwerp in 1549: Renaissance and Mannerist Architecture in the Low Countries from 1530 to 1630.* 2 vols. Leyden, 1994, pp. 150–73.

AUGSBURG, THE FUGGER CHAPEL

Bruno Bushart. *Die Fuggerkapelle bei St. Anna in Augsburg.* Munich, 1994.

Andrew Morrall. *Jörg Breu the Elder: Art, Culture and Belief in Reformation Augsburg.* Aldershot et al., 2001.

BELÉM

Jochen Staebel. 'Navis Ecclesiae Militantis': Zur Schiffsallegorie in der emanuelinischen Baukunst'. In Barbara Hüttel et al. (eds). *Revisionen: Zur Aktualität von Kunstgeschichte.* Berlin, 2002, pp. 77–96.

Paulo Pereira, 'Reais quinas' la propaganda regia, l'architettura e l'iconologia del potere al tempo di Don Manuel'. In Arturo Calzona et al. (eds). *Il Principe Architetto.* Florence, 2002, pp. 545–63.

BLOIS

Brigitte Walbe. 'Frühe Architektur-Fotografie in Frankreich am Beispiel des Schlosses von Blois'. *Marburger Jahrbuch für Kunstwissenschaft* 20 (1981), pp. 63–71.

Marc Hamilton Smith. 'François Ier, l'Italie et le Château de Blois: nouveaux documents, nouvelles dates'. *Bulletin monumental* 147 (1989), pp. 307–23.

Matthias Müller. 'Capriccio oder Politikum? Überlegungen zu ungewöhnlichen Treppentürmen an deutschen und französischen Renaissanceschlössern'. In Lutz Unbehaun et al. (eds). *Die Künste und das Schloss in der Frühen Neuzeit.* Munich, 1998, pp. 131–49.

BRUGES, THE OLD REGISTRY

Luc Devliegher. *Beeld van het kunstbezit. Inleiding tot een Inventarisatie.* Tielt, 1965.

Memling und seine Zeit: Memlingmuseum Brügge. Exh. cat. Stuttgart, 1998.

BURGHLEY HOUSE

Charles Read. *Lord Burghley and Queen Elizabeth.* London, 1960.

Mark Girouard. 'Elizabethan Architecture and the Gothic Tradition'. *Architectural History* 6 (1963), pp. 23–40.

Jill Husselby. 'The Politics of Pleasure: William Cecil and Burghley House'. In Pauline Croft (ed.). *Patronage, Culture, and Power: The Early Cecils, 1558–1612.* New Haven, CT, and London, 2002, pp. 21–45.

COLOGNE

Michael Keine. 'Nach- und Neugotik an der Cologneer Rathauslaube'. In Walter Geis and Ulrich Krings (eds). *Köln: Das gotische Rathaus und seine historische Umgebung.* Cologne 2000, pp. 509–27.

CHAMBORD

Jean Guillaume. 'Léonard de Vinci et l'architecture française: I, Le Problème de Chambord'. *Revue de l'Art* 25 (1974), pp. 71–84.

Wolfgang Metternich. *Schloss Chambord an der Loire: Der Bau von 1519–1524*. Darmstadt, 1985.

Hidemichi Tanaka, 'Leonardo da Vinci: Architect of Chambord'. *Artibus et Historiae* 25 (1992), pp. 85–102.

Monique Chatenet. *Chambord*. Paris, 2001.

CRACOW CATHEDRAL, SIGISMUND CHAPEL

Stanislaw Mossakowski. 'Bartolomeo Berecci à Cracovice: La chapelle Sigismond'. *Revue de l'art* 101 (1993), pp. 67–85.

CRACOW, THE WAWEL

Helena Kosakiewicz and Stefan Kosakiewicz. *The Renaissance in Poland*. Warsaw, 1976.

Dietmar Popp and Robert Suckale (eds). *Die Jagiellonen: Kunst und Kultur einer europäischen Dynastie an der Wende zur Neuzeit*. Nuremberg, 2002.

EL ESCORIAL

George A. Kubler. *Building the Escorial*. Princeton, NJ, 1982.

Catherine Wilkinson-Zerner. *Juan de Herrera: Architect to Philip II of Spain*. New Haven, CT, 1993.

ESZTERGOM

Jolán Balogh. 'La Capella Bakócz in Esztergom'. *Acta Historiae Artium* 3 (1956), pp. 1–197.

Matthias Corvinus und die Renaissance in Ungarn 1458–1541. Exh. cat. Schallaburg, 1982.

Miklós Horler. *The Bakócz Chapel of Esztergom Cathedral*. Budapest, 1990.

Gyöngyi Török. 'Die Ursprünge der jagiellonischen Renaissance in Ungarn während der Regierungszeit des Königs Matthias Corvinus (1458–1490)'. In Dietmar Popp and Robert Suckale (eds). *Die Jagiellonen: Kunst und Kultur einer europäischen Dynastie an der Wende zur Neuzeit*. Nuremberg, 2002, pp. 215–26.

FLORENCE, PALAZZO MEDICI

Giovanni Cherubini and Giovanni Fanelli (eds). *Il Palazzo Medici Riccardi di Firenze*. Florence, 1990.

Andreas Tönnesmann. 'Zwischen Bürgerhaus und Residenz: Zur sozialen Typik des Palazzo Medici'. In Andreas Beyer and Bruce Boucher (eds). *Piero de'Medici 'il Gottoso' (1416–1469): Kunst im Dienste der Mediceer*. Berlin, 1993, pp. 71–88.

FLORENCE, PALAZZO PITTI

Andreas Tönnesmann. *Der Palazzo Gondi in Florenz*. Worms, 1983.

Michael Keine. *Bartolomeo Ammannati*. Milan, 1995.

FLORENCE, PALAZZO STROZZI

Palazzo Strozzi metà millennio 1489–1989. Rome, 1991.

Alexander Markschies. *Gebaute Pracht: Der Palazzo Strozzi in Florenz (1489–1534)*. Freiburg im Breisgau, 2000.

FONTAINEBLEAU

Françoise Boudon, Jean Blécon and Catherine Grodecki. *Le Château de Fontainebleau de François Ier à Henri IV: Les Bâtiments et leurs fonctions*. Paris, 1998.

Jean-Marie Pérouse de Montclos. *Fontainebleau*. Paris, 1998.

GDAŃSK

Arnold Bartetzky. *Das grosse Zeughaus in Danzig: Baugeschichte, Architekturgeschichtliche Stellung, Repräsentative Funktion*. Stuttgart, 2000.

GRANADA CATHEDRAL

Earl Edgar Rosenthal. *The Cathedral of Granada: A Study in the Spanish Renaissance*. Princeton, NJ, 1961.

GRANADA, PALACE OF CHARLES V

Earl Edgar Rosenthal. *The Palace of Charles V in Granada*. Princeton, NJ, 1985.

Manfredo Tafuri. 'La Granada di Carlo V.: Il palazzo, il mausoleo'. In idem, *Ricerca del Rinascimento: Principi, Città, Architetti*. Turin, 1992, pp. 255–304.

HAMPTON COURT

Simon Thurley. *The Royal Palaces of Tudor England: Architecture and Court Life 1460–1547*. New Haven, CT, and London 1993.

Jonathan Foyle. 'A Reconstruction of Thomas Wolsey's Great Hall at Hampton Court Palace'. *Architectural History* 45 (2002), pp. 128–58.

HEIDELBERG CASTLE

Hanns Hubach and Volker Sellin. *Heidelberg: Das Schloss*. Heidelberg, 1995.

Hanns Hubach. 'Kurfürst Ottheinrich als Hercules Palatinus: Vorbemerkungen zur Ikonographie des Figurenzyklus' an der Fassade des Ottheinrichbaus im Heidelberger Schloss'. In *Pfalzgraf Ottheinrich: Politik, Kunst und Wissenschaft im 16. Jahrhundert*. Regensburg, 2002, pp. 231–48.

HELMSTEDT

Harmen Thies. *Das Juleum Novum: Paul Francke*. Helmstedt, 1997 (Beiträge zur Geschichte des Landkreises und der ehemaligen Universität Helmstedt, no. 9).

LANDSHUT RESIDENCE

Iris Lauterbach et al. (ed.). *Die Landshuter Stadtresidenz: Architektur und Ausstattung*. Munich, 1998.

MECHELN

Dagmar Eichberger. *Leben mit Kunst, Wirken durch Kunst: Sammelwesen und Hofkunst unter Margarete von Österreich, Regentin der Niederlande*. Turnhout, 2002.

MOSCOW

'Aristotele Fioravanti a Mosca: Convegno sugli Architetti italiani del Rinascimento in Russia'. *Arte Lombarda* 44/45 (1976).

MUNICH, HALL OF ANTIQUITIES, THE RESIDENCE

Ellen Weski, Heike Frosien-Leinz and Wolf-Dieter Grimm. *Das Antiquarium der Münchner Residenz: Katalog der Skulpturen*. Munich, 1987.

Um Glauben und Reich: Wittelsbach und Bayern. Ed. Hubert Glaser. Exh. cat. Munich and Zurich, 1980.

Dorothea Diemer and Peter Diemer. 'Das Antiquarium Herzog Albrechts v. von Bayern: Schicksale einer fürstlichen Antikensammlung der Spätrenaissance'. *Zeitschrift für Kunstgeschichte* 58 (1995), pp. 55–104.

MUNICH, JESUIT CHURCH OF ST MICHAEL

Norbert Huse. *Kleine Kunstgeschichte Münchens*. Munich, 1990.

Reinhold Baumstark (ed.). *Rom in Bayern: Kunst und Spiritualität der ersten Jesuiten*. Munich, 1997.

PARIS, SAINT-EUSTACHE

Anne-Marie Sankovitch. 'A Reconsideration of French Renaissance Church Architecture'. In Jean Guillaume (ed.). *L'Eglise dans l'Architecture de la Renaissance*. Paris, 1995, pp. 161–80.

——. 'Structure/ornament and the Modern Figuration of Architecture'. *The Art Bulletin* 80 (1998), pp. 687–717.

PIENZA

Charles Randall Mack, *Pienza: The Creation of a Renaissance City*. Ithaca, NY, and London, 1987.

Andreas Tönnesmann. *Pienza: Städtebau und Humanismus*. Munich, 1990.

Jan Pieper. *Pienza: Der Entwurf einer humanistischen Weltsicht*. Stuttgart and London, 1997.

PONZNAŃ

Witold Maisel. 'Giovanni Battista Quadro e le sue opere in Polonia'. *Palladio* 15 (1965), pp. 111–28.

Mariusz Karpowicz. *Artisti ticinesi in Polonia nel '500*. Canobbio and Lugano, 1987, pp. 97–130.

Arnold Bartetzky. 'Stadt und Königtum: Frühneuzeitliche Rathausdekorationen in Polen als politische Zeugnisse'. In Dietmar Popp and Robert Suckale (eds). *Die Jagiellonen: Kunst und Kultur einer europäischen Dynastie an der Wende zur Neuzeit*. Nuremberg, 2002, pp. 73–84.

PRAGUE, THE BELVEDERE

Jirina Hőřésí et al. *Die Kunst der Renaissance und des Manierismus in Böhmen*. Prague, 1979.

Ferdinand Seibt (ed.). *Renaissance in Böhmen*. Munich, 1985.

PRAGUE, HRADČANY

Götz Fehr. *Benedikt Ried: Ein deutscher Baumeister zwischen Gotik und Renaissance in Böhmen*. Munich, 1961.

PRAGUE, VILLA HVEZDA

Jarmila Krčálová. *Centrální stavby české renesance*. Prague, 1976.

Christian Gries. 'Erzherzog Ferdinand von Tirol: Konturen einer Sammlerpersönlichkeit'. *Frühneuzeit-Info* 4 (1993), pp. 162–73.

ROME, IL GESÙ

James S. Ackerman. 'The Gesù in the Light of Contemporary Church Design'. In Rudolf Wittkower and Irma B. Jaffe (eds). *Baroque Art: The Jesuit Contribution*. New York 1972, pp. 15–28.

Klaus Schwager. 'La chiesa del Gesù del Vignola'. *Bollettino del Centro Internazionale di Studi di Architettura Andrea Palladio* 19 (1977), pp. 251–71.

Klaus Schwager. 'L'Architecture religieuse à Rome de Pie IV à Clément VIII'. In Jean Guillaume (ed.). *L'Eglise dans l'architecture de la Renaissance*. Paris, 1995, pp. 223–42.

ROME, PALAZZO DELLA CANCELLERIA

Christoph Luitpold Frommel. *Der römische Palast der Hochrenaissance*. Tübingen, 1973.

Christoph Luitpold Frommel. 'Raffaele Riario, committente della Cancelleria'. In Arnold Esch et al. (eds). *Arte, Committenza ed Economia a Roma e nelle Corti del Rinascimento*. Turin, 1995, pp. 197–211.

ROME, PALAZZO FARNESE

Le Palais Farnèse. Rome, 1981.

ROME, ST PETER'S

Franz Graf Wolff Metternich and Christof Thoenes. *Die frühen St.-Peter-Entwürfe*. Tübingen, 1987.

Achim Arbeiter. *Alt-St. Peter in Geschichte und Wissenschaft*. Berlin, 1988.

Cristiano Tessari (ed.). *San Pietro che non c'è*. Milan, 1996.

Horst Bredekamp. *Sankt Peter in Rom und das Prinzip der produktiven Zerstörung: Bau und Abbau von Bramante bis Bernini*. Berlin, 2000.

ROME, VILLA FARNESINA

Christoph Luitpold Frommel. *Die Farnesina und Peruzzis römisches Frühwerk*. Berlin, 1961.

Sonja Müller. *Palast- und Villenbau in Siena um 1500: Studien zur Entwicklung der sienesischen Renaissancearchitektur*. Darmstadt, 1999.

Andreas Tönnesmann. *Kleine Kunstgeschichte Roms*. Munich, 2002.

TODI, SANTA MARIA DELLA CONSOLAZIONE

Jürgen Zänker. *Die Wallfahrtskirche Santa Maria Consolazione in Todi*. Bonn, 1971.

Arnoldo Bruschi. *Il Tempio della Consolazione a Todi*. Milan, 1991.

TORGAU

Hans-Joachim Krause. 'Die Emporenanlage der Torgauer Schlosskapelle in ihrer ursprünglichen Gestalt und Funktion'. In *Bau- und Bildkunst im Spiegel internationaler Forschung*. Berlin, 1989, pp. 233–45.

Stephan Hoppe. *Die funktionale und räumliche Struktur des frühen Schlossbaus in Mitteldeutschland: Untersucht an Beispielen landesherrlicher Bauten der Zeit zwischen 1470–1570*. Cologne, 1996.

Matthias Müller. 'Das Schloss als fürstliches Manifest: Zur Architekturmetaphorik in den wettinischen Residenzschlössern von Meissen und Torgau'. In Jörg Rogge and Uwe Schirmer (eds). *Hochadlige Herrschaft im mitteldeutschen Raum*. Leipzig, 2002, pp.

URBINO

Pasquale Rotondi. *The Ducal Palace of Urbino: Its Architecture and Decoration*. London, 1969.

Andreas Tönnesmann. 'Il Palazzo Ducale di Urbino: economia e committenza'. In Arnold Esch (ed.). *Arte, Committenza ed Economia a Roma e nelle Corti del Rinascimento*. Turin, 1995, pp. 399–411.

Werner Lutz. *Luciano Laurana und der Herzogspalast von Urbino*. Weimar, 1995.

VENICE, ST MARK'S SQUARE

Deborah Howard. *Jacopo Sansovino: Architecture and Patronage in Renaissance Venice*. New Haven, CT, London, 1975.

Thomas Hirthe. *Il 'Foro all'Antica' di Venezia: La Trasformazione di Piazza San Marco nel Cinquecento*. Venice, 1986.

Manuela Morresi. *Jacopo Sansovino*. Milan, 2000.

VENICE, SANTA, MARIA DEI MIRACOLI

Ralph Lieberman. *The Church of Santa Maria dei Miracoli in Venice*. New York and London, 1986.

Wolfgang Wolters. *Architektur und Ornament: Venezianischer Bauschmuck der Renaissance*. Munich, 2000.

Index of Place Names

Photographic Credits

Every effort has been made to acknowledge respective
copyright owners. In some cases, however, it has not
been possible to trace ownership. The Publisher would
be pleased to hear from such persons so that an
amendment can be made in future editions.
Numbers refer to pages.
t = top, b = bottom, l = left, r = right, c = centre

akg-images: 73 b r, 82 t, 98, 119 b l; Cameraphoto 81 b; Erich
Lessing 89 b c; Pirozzi 37 b r; Rabatti-Domingie 71 t r, b, 113 c
l, 115 b l; Schütze/Rodemann 121 b
Archivi Alinari, Florence: 27 t, 33 b l, 91 b r, 113 b l; G. Tatge 17 t
artur, Cologne: Archiv Archipress 97 t; Markus Bassler/Mon-
heim 75 t; Klaus Frahm 17 b r, 25 t, b, 57 b c; Reinhard Görner
131 b l, b r; Lisa Hammel/Monheim 103 t; Jochen Helle 125 t;
Florian Monheim 62/63 (and back cover b c), 64 b l, b c; Monheim & von Götz 85 b r; Monika Nikolic 81 t, c l, c r
Bartetzky, Arnold 13
Achim Bednorz, Cologne: 15 b l, 21, 23 b l, 29 t, 34 b r, 35, 42 b
r, 43, 45 t (and back cover t l), 45 b l, 52 b l, 53 (and back cover t
c), 63 c l, 72/73, 73 b r, 79 t, b l, 91 c r, 95 b l, b c, b r, 99 b r, 123
t, 129 b r
Bibliotheca Hertziana, Rome: 37 b l
Bilderberg, Hamburg: Felipe J. Alcoceba 118/119; Milan Hora-
cek 92/93; Reinhart Wolf 121 t
Bridgeman Art Library, London: 19 b r, 71 t l, 73 c r, 99 t, 111;
Mark Fiennes 107 t, b c, b r
Jutta Brüdern, Brunswick: 133 (and back cover t r)
Achim Bunz, Munich: 127 t, b r, 131 t
Department Monuments and Sites, Brussels: Oswald Pauwels
51 t, 87 t (and back cover b r)
Getty Images/Stone, Munich: Pascal Crapet 77 t
Herbert Hartmannn, Munich: 23 t, b r
Helikon Verlag, Budapest: 49
Markus Hilbich, Berlin: 41 t, 47, 55 b l, b r, 57 b r, 61 b l, 67, 100,
109 b l, b r, 125 b
Angelo Hornak, London: 107 b l, 139 t
Bildagentur Huber, Garmisch-Partenkirchen: Giovanni 97 b r;
Gräfenhain 119 c r; R. Schmid 101, 105 t; Giovanni Simeone
109 t; Simeone 113 b r, 129 t
IFA-Bilderteam, Ottobrunn: Aberham 44 b r; Diaf 69 b r, 97 b
l; Kohlhas 117 t; Walter Strobl 15 b, TPC 31 t; Vahl 95 t
Volkmar Janicke, Munich: 135 b l
Architektur-Bilderservice Kandula, Witten: Stefan Drechsel 85
b c, 93 b; Stanislaus Kandula 137 t; Hans P. Szyszka 85 t, b l
laif, Cologne: Achim Gaasterland 83 t, 115 t; Gonzalez 79 b r;
Manfred Linke 69 c l; Anna Neumann 75 b; Andreas Hub 137
b; Zanettini 45 b r
Alexander Langkals, Landshut: front cover
LOOK, Munich: Karl Johaentges 83 b l, b r;
Rainer Martini 91 t
Alexander Markschies, Aachen: 51 b, 87 b
Paolo Marton, Treviso: 15 b r
Bildarchiv Monheim, Meerbusch: Florian Monheim 65 (and
back cover b l)
Werner Neumeister, Munich: 31 c, b r, 41 b r, 58, 59 l, r, 89 t,
103 b l, b r
Toni Ott, Landshut: 89 b l, b c
PhotoPress, Stockdorf: Jasiak 135 t; Leidorf 55 t
Hildegard Rupeks-Wolter, Berlin: 31 b l
Archivio Scala, Florence (Antella): frontispiece; 17 b l, 19 t, b l,
27 b l, b r, 29 b, 33 t, b c, 37 t, 39 t, b r, 57 t, b l, 61 t, b r, 63 b r,
77 b l, 113 t, 115 b r, 119 b r, 129 b l
Stadtgeschichtliches Museum Leipzig: 105 b r
Peter Stepan, Munich: 68/69
Martin Thomas, Aachen: 7 b, 139 b r